FRENCH PROVINCIAL
DECORATIVE ART

FRENCH PROVINCIAL
DECORATIVE ART

By

Catharine Oglesby

BONANZA BOOKS, NEW YORK

This edition published by Bonanza Books,
a division of Crown Publishers, Inc.,
by arrangement with Charles Scribner's Sons.
(A)

Appreciation

For an American to attempt to present the decorative arts of Provincial France is audacious. But I was encouraged in my project by the fact that the best book on French Provincial Architecture was written by two Americans—Goodwin and Milliken—and because the French themselves are still enamored of the glories of their palaces.

It would be impossible to mention the names of all the persons who have helped me in this study of the decorative arts of Old France. My introduction to them occurred many years ago in the galleries of John Wanamaker, New York, where I saw the selections made by three women of superb taste, Mrs. Tyson, Ruby Ross Wood and Nancy McClelland. It was Dorothy Shaver, president of Lord and Taylor, who persuaded me to buy my first piece of French Provincial furniture—a Régence commode. That purchase launched me on a quest that has carried me across oceans and continents and has never ended.

In my pursuit of the products of French Provincial craftsmen, I was fortunate to meet Josephine Howell. Her eclectic taste, and her relentless stress on quality, was a challenge and an inspiration for which I shall be ever grateful and then, too, she introduced me to the charm of French faïence. Jacques Helft graciously permitted me to study his collection of 18th Century silver and often, when I was overtaken by pangs of humility and economy, spurred me on to continued study and acquisition. To my friend, Elinor Merrell, I am indebted for many instructive hours spent with her fabrics, books and ornaments. Her warm appreciation of these old arts and crafts, and her interpretations of them given with a brief gesture, a short word, put spectacles on my eyes.

Curators of museums, antiquaries and booksellers in Rouen, Paris, Bourges, Tours,

v

APPRECIATION

Blois, Limoges, Clermont-Ferrand, Lyons, Dijon, Arles, Avignon, and many other cities and villages in France, aided my study with their learning and courtesy. They will be first to recognize and to condone my errors and omissions because knowledge is kind.

Mme. Marcelle Tredolat and Mr. Helmer MacIntosh of R. H. Macy & Company, Paris, furthered my trips, and most helpful was M. Henri Cabanne, who is a Sherlock at discovering the hidden and inaccessible, and who never groaned beneath my bundles, though he did waver when, one hot day in Arles, I suggested, "Now let's collect *doors.*"

I am deeply indebted to the staff of The Metropolitan Museum of Art, The Cooper Union Museum of Decorative Art, The Parke-Bernet Galleries, and French & Co., of New York; to Dr. Oswald Goetz of The Art Institute of Chicago, Ill.; to Mr. Edger Richardson of The Detroit Institute of Arts, Detroit, Mich.; to Miss Ethel M. Pinkerton of The Montreal Museum of Fine Arts, Montreal, Canada; and especially to Miss Bernice Baumgarten, whose ability and faith ushered my work to this conclusion.

There still remains those to whom my greatest debt is due—the known and unknown, Ornamentalists and Craftsmen of Old France.

CATHARINE OGLESBY.

Contents

CONTENTS

FRENCH PROVINCIAL
DECORATIVE ART

CHAPTER I

French Provincial Design

A NEW design was born in France two centuries ago. Today it is called "French Provincial". Unique and fortunate circumstances attended its birth and promoted its development. Though sponsored by kings and fostered by wealth, it was a product of the people. Aristocratic in birth and breeding, it was democratic in being. Genius and fame contributed to its flowering, but it matured under the hands of anonymous craftsmen, and its harbor was not the palace, but the home.

This design was the result of two forces. For many years there had existed a group of Guilds whose membership was drawn from the trades. The Guilds were founded on a system of apprenticeship. The requirements were strict and operations were rigorously policed. Men took pride in the quality of their materials and the excellence of their execution. Mind, hand and eye were trained to beauty and achievement. Integrity in spirit, thought and performance was dominant.

In this rich soil a germ was suddenly planted by a King. Louis XIV concentrated the creative talent of the nation on the decorative arts. The desire for beautiful furnishings took possession of France. The owner might have a sumptuous hotel in Paris, or a manor or a farm in the Provinces, he might wish for tapestries or homespuns; it was the same desire that motivated both acquisitions. A fury of production stimulated the creative artist to draw, paint, design everything from a picture to a chair, a statue to a candlestick. Their originations might have remained nothing more than lines on paper had it not been for the fact that the Guilds had developed a corps of craftsmen who were capable of rendering them adequately.

1

A flood of magnificent furnishings entered the great palaces of France and the King and his court wanted more and more. The same acquisitive spirit was rampant in the homes throughout the nation. For them the craftsmen produced furnishings which possessed a merit all their own. To understand how this could be, one must consider the unique character of the French people.

Though much has been written about the luxurious courts of France, its kings and their favorites, the *salt* of France was never to be found in the great palaces of Paris, Versailles, Fontainebleau. It existed in the little homes of France scattered throughout her provinces. For France is a land of towns and farms, not cities; of homes, not palaces. And the people who made these homes created them in their own likeness.

The land of France has seabound, rocky coasts bordering the Atlantic. Sun-warmed, flower-starred fields along the Mediterranean. Cold, mountainous plateaux and broad plains, where waving fields of grain mature to rich harvest. The people who lived in these different sections had the same characteristics as their land. There was the austere Breton, the gay Provençal, the valiant mountain-folk and the staunch people of the grain-lands. All were ardent individualists. They appreciated the genuine; disliked bombast and pretension. They sought freedom of imagination, enjoyed invention, thrilled to discovery. They knew that happiness is born of order. That etiquette and convention enrich rather than constrict. They were a family people who would share their happiness, and the home was the center of their life.

In Old France, two kinds of homes were built; the manors of the well-to-do and the cottages of the farmers and town-folk. To furnish them, two types of furnishings were made by local craftsmen.

There was the simple, farm-house type termed "mobilier rustique". The word "rustique" cannot be accurately translated because this word infers a degree of crudeness which is not always present in the products themselves. The "rustique" resembles in feeling the Early American and Shaker types. The furnishings termed "art regional" were made by local craftsmen in the various parts of France for the homes and manors of the rich nobility and prosperous bourgeoisie. They have the vigor, but also the refinement, of the furnishings of the American Federal Period. These two types had one characteristic in common: both stemmed from the pattern set by the Kings of France. They echo the line, structure and design of palace furnishings but interpret the basic pattern with simpler materials and less ornament.

The name, coined in America, for these two types of furniture is "French Provincial", which literally means "made in the provinces of France" and is quite apt. For during the 17th and 18th Centuries the sections of France in which this furniture was

2

Fig. 1 Drawing room of the Early 18th Century Showing Pan-
elled Walls of Walnut, Marble Mantel with Overmantel
Mirror, Parquet Floor. Now in the Metropolitan Museum of
Art, New York City

produced were called "provinces"; since the 19th Century they have been called "Departments".

The term "Provincial" is sometimes confused with the word "Provençal". The error is a natural one to make because the difference in spelling and pronunciation between the two words is slight and the craftsmen of Provénce, a beautiful state in southeastern France, were exceptionally gifted and prolific. However, to confine French Provincial Design to the output of this one section is to deprive ourselves of a wealth of beauty. And though the French themselves may be confused by our coined-phrase "French Provincial" it is good because it is inclusive enough to provide a name for all the products made for the homes of the middle-class during the late 17th, the 18th and early 19th Centuries in all the provinces of Old France.

Gracious, charming, but practical and sturdy, these French Provincial Furnishings answer every demand of home-life. Style and distinction are present but always guided by suitability to purpose and place. Their design is invariably marked by good taste without ostentation. They preserve their essential function, but to it is added grace and charm. Their scale is happy in home-size surroundings and use enhances their beauty.

French chairs are comfortable. Even the small, straight side chairs are so proportioned as to fit the back with ease, and their pitch gives just the right support and play to feet and legs. Men, stern testers of chairs and comfort, approve of them. The variety of little tables answers the need for lamps, books, vases. The hanging shelves on which to display ornaments delight the collector in every one. The buffets and cupboards solve the need for storage space in a decorative and convenient fashion.

Textiles are blessed with a wealth of invention in design, a choice consideration of color. Under the hands of the Provincial craftsmen, wool becomes amiable and cotton assumes chic. But it is the decorative accessories that are truly delightful. Whether fashioned of clay, wood or metal, they are created with such an eye to beauty and variety as to permit individual taste free play and satisfactory expression.

The products of the craftsmen of the provinces of Old France will be enjoyed more, if, to their visual satisfaction is added that of knowing how—when—why—they were born. Though inspired by the Kings and their courts, they are an expression of a people who loved their homes. They mirror the experiences of a race. Tastes may change and the needs of today be ended by the riches of tomorrow but fine proportion and fine craftsmanship present a human quality that transcends time. The heritage of beauty created in the provinces of Old France has enriched the lives of many generations and is destined to contribute bounteously to those that are yet to come.

4

CHAPTER II

France Builds Homes

HEN you motor along a winding country road and, looking out over the far vista of green meadows and tall trees, see perking up here and there like poppies in a cornfield, little homes in the building, you can easily imagine what France was like in the early years of the 17th Century.

Peace was newly come after centuries of strife. For decades the pillaging armies of Germany, Italy and Spain had traversed the nation. Later the soldiery of feudal lords passed to and fro—robbing, burning, destroying the land that they battled to possess. Then came the religious wars, and civil strife is the worst of all. While armies were passing hither and yon, the people were too much occupied with saving their skins to think of owning more than they had on their backs. But now, fear, which had bound men together for protection, was discarded, like the cast-off chrysalis of a butterfly. Men stood erect, free, individual.

Content, in the past, to hope for the reward of his deeds in the next world, the Frenchman now wanted to enjoy the fruits of his industry in this world. France had already achieved great architecture. But the medieval chateaux of kings and nobles were actually forts for combat and refuge. Great Gothic cathedrals pierced the sky with their spires, but they had been built by the group. Now the religion of the Frenchman spurned superstition; he expected it to be expressed not merely in prayers, but in deeds. He wanted not only to build, but to possess. He wanted a home, a wife by the hearth to spin, sew, embroider and to plan the dowry chests of his daughters and the future of his sons. Now, at last, the turmoil subsided; peace arrived; prosperity was due, when in 1589 a great and good King, Henry IV, came to the throne of a united France.

Inspired by their King, assured by the newly come peace, an orgy of building enveloped the nation. Rivers were opened to navigation, canals were constructed, roads were built. And motoring today through France you may ride under arches of great elms for in the days of Henry IV no road was completed until an avenue of elms was planted along it . . . an idea contemporary roadmakers might well copy. Secure from religious and civil strife, villages now sprang up along the canals and rivers, and little houses clustered near the new bridges and crossroads.

North and south, the home was one large room. This was used for eating, cooking and sleeping. In the mountainous regions the stable was placed under this main room. The heat of the animals' bodies helped to warm the main room during cold nights, but in the warmer climates the animals were kept in a lean-to. When the finances of the family permitted, a second room was added. It became a bedroom, the first room continuing to be living room, dining room and kitchen. Since food and warmth were the two prime requirements, the fireplace was an important feature of the room and its size increased or decreased according to the temperature of the locality in which it was built. The four walls of the house served as follows: the door or entrance wall, the fireplace, the cabinet, and the bed-wall. In the center, before the fireplace, the table, chairs and stools were placed.

There were no furniture stores or shops, since only the King and his nobles had household possessions, and these were imported or custom-built. So it was natural for the owner of a new home to turn for help to the men who built his house. These builders were of two professions—the "joiner" who knew the art of putting wood together and the "turner" who knew how to shape the wood. Eventually, as business prospered, these men formed two groups: the "Joiners Guild", whose members made cabinets and beds; the "Turners Guild", who made chairs and tables. Thus was born the great furniture industry of France.

The source of the new style of home furnishings was in the countries which bounded France—Italy, Germany, Flanders, Spain. For two centuries Italian architects, artisans, artists, sculptors, metalists and weavers had been imported into France to build and to decorate the palaces of the Kings and his nobles. They brought to the

6

Fig. 2 Drawing for a 17th Century Textile Showing Life of the Provincials

court of France the influence of Italy which had achieved the glory of its Renaissance when France was but a crude upstart nation devoid of taste or manners. Consequently, the architecture and furnishings of the large homes of 17th Century France reflected the influence of their more cultured neighbor, Italy.

To the north of France lay Flanders and Germany, linked to France's southern neighbor, Spain, by the intermarriage of its rulers. During the time of Henry IV and Louis XIII, Spain was at the zenith of its power and Flanders was staging a culture made glorious by Rubens, Van Dyke and a host of famous artisans. While the palaces of the French Kings continued to be dominated by the taste of Italy, the styles of Flanders and of Germany were ascendant in the "little homes" of France.

7

One of the peculiarities of the French temperament, and one most difficult to understand, is its combination of the conservative and the revolutionary. Above all else, the Frenchman is an individualist of amazing creative impulse. When he set out to beautify his home, he accepted the tutorship of his more accomplished neighbors which was sponsored by his Kings, but he expressed himself in his own way. Just as he evolved a language of his own, so when he worked in wood, fabric, ceramics, metal, these materials acquired a distinct and characteristic style—definitely and unmistakably French. In the cottages and manors of old France a new style of decorative art was born. It was destined to become one of the most charming and individual expressions of beauty in every-day life that our civilization has known. For the next three centuries the taste of France was to dominate, inspire, and to be copied by every country of Europe. And in this 20th Century it was again to flower in America.

Fig. 3 Cabinet Makers Shop. Diderot et d' Alembert Encyclopedia 1776

CHAPTER III

Styles, Times and Kings

HE 17th Century marked the beginning of decorative art in the homes of France. It was destined to flourish with increasing vigor during three centuries. Pure monarchy was established. The authority of the King was supreme throughout the nation and all intellectual movement, fine arts and decorative crafts proceeded from the court. The styles of furnishings produced during these three centuries are known by the names of the rulers of France who reigned during these years. They were:

Henry IV	1589-1610
Louis XIII	1610-1643
Louis XIV	1643-1715
The Regent	1715-1723
Louis XV	1715-1774
Louis XVI	1774-1793
The Directory	1795-1799
Napoleon I	1799-1814

However, the importance of the *Period* in French Provincial furnishings is often over-emphasized and frequently misunderstood. The terms "Style Louis XV", and

"Style Louis XVI", et cetera, do not refer solely to the time of making but rather these terms are chronological. The heavily carved Louis XIV style pre-dated the gracious rococo style named after Louis XV and this was followed by the straight line which characterizes the style known as Louis XVI. Actually, these various styles of furniture overlapped the reigns of these Kings and all of these period-styles were produced far into the 19th Century, for after the death of her Kings the French seemed to have lost their stimulus. They continued to produce but without innovation.

THE STYLE HENRY IV AND LOUIS XIII (1589-1643)

King Henry was a red-blooded, forthright soldier who fought his way to the throne. He became a great pacifier and united the Roman Catholic and Huguenot parties which had long been at war. A master of the art of pleasing, Henry was a bit too much given to gallantry. Judicious and far-sighted in dealing with the enemies of the nation, he was sagacious and sympathetic to the trouble-makers in his state. "Paris is worth a mass," he is said to have gaily announced when he consented to become a Catholic, but beneath this nonchalance he was resolved that Protestants should worship in their own way. Responsive to his people, the chosen slogan of his reign was, "I want all my peasantry to have a fowl in the pot every Sunday."

Henry, "le Vert Gallant", as he was fondly named, was like many men you know— a genius at his business but a fool in his bedroom. He could make and keep a peace between creeds and nations, but peace in his home he never knew. Early in his reign he married a "fat bankeress from Florence"—Marie de Medici—tall, pop-eyed, cantankerous, deceitful, frowsy, stupid—to whom he once wrote, "God's life, my love, you could not have sent me more agreeable news than that you have taken to reading."

Queen Marie loved royalty for its pomp. She was an ardent devotee of the culture of Flanders. However, in 1601 the "fat bankeress" justified herself to France by presenting her husband with a son who became Louis XIII. He was as homely as his father was handsome, as taciturn as his sire was talkative, as lazy as Henry was industrious, and as ascetic as his gallant parent was amorous. His chief interest was in riding and hunting but he was a man of taste, a painter, a student. He chose as his prime minister, Cardinal Richelieu, who consolidated the peace established by Henry IV.

Louis XIII married Ann of Austria, a beautiful Spanish princess, who some say was lazy and selfish, but others say was much maligned. After her husband's death, she is presumed to have married (no proof exists) her prime minister, Cardinal Mazarin. The two prime ministers, Richelieu and Mazarin, were men who loved luxurious living. Whatever may be said about their methods and morals, they steered the nation toward

Fig. 4 Louis XIV Dining Room in Miniature by Mrs. James Ward Thorne

peace, unity, international respect, and their rule introduced a stable, productive prosperity into the homes of the French.

Thus the 17th Century began everything, finished nothing, but it produced the great men who opened the door to the future of France as a center of culture.

Henry IV was a soldier, his son a frugal King, and the spirit of these monarchs is evidenced by the furniture produced during their reigns. It is strong, massive, direct, obviously influenced by the Italian, Spanish and Flemish furnishings which were imported for the new palaces of the Kings and their Prime Ministers and slavishly copied by the members of the court.

11

The forms are square and architectural. The carvings are large in scale and deep in cutting. The woods are dark of tone. The upholstery was chiefly leather and wool and these used but sparingly. The French craftsman was yet to discover his own genius.

THE STYLE LOUIS XIV (1643-1715)

When Louis XIV mounted the throne of France in 1643 he was thought to be only an indolent, ignorant, young fellow who would never amount to very much. For years he idled away his time with adolescent lovemaking, games, hunting and ballet dancing. He seemed quite content to permit his prime minister, Cardinal Mazarin, to manage the affairs of the nation. The court was rife with feuds as noble maneuvered noble to gain power and wealth. The young King said nothing but he watched the jealous, selfish activities of the lords of his realm and he never again trusted them. When Mazarin died, Louis XIV had reached manhood and he electrified his court and country by assuming the full powers of an absolute monarch which he expressed in his historic announcement, "I am the state."

The easy-going lad suddenly became a strict disciplinarian, an imperious, ambitious sovereign, resolved that France was to be the greatest country of the world. And he accomplished his purpose magnificently. Under the rule of Louis XIV France reached the zenith of her power. She became the leading nation of Europe. The reign of Louis the Grand was the longest, the most brilliant, of any French King. The impetus for this spectacular achievement in war, industry and art, proceeded from the King.

Among the many titles which Louis XIV assumed upon his accession to the throne was that of "protector of science, literature and art". There was none that he valued more highly. Determined to perpetuate the glory of France, Louis sought out the men who were capable of aiding him in the achievement of his purpose.

Two of the great geniuses appointed by Louis XIV were Colbert, who became Minister of Finance and established the Gobelins Industry, and Le Brun, who managed this stupendous enterprise. The Gobelins Manufactures was more than a factory, it was a school where every branch of the arts, both fine and decorative, was practised— painting, sculpture, architecture, cabinet-making, tapestry weaving, leather-dressing, gold- and silversmithy. Under the inspired leadership of Le Brun, the fine and decorative arts were, for the first time, united. The purpose and accomplishment of every artist and craftsman were dedicated to the glory of the King and France. The crowning achievement made by this King, his minister, and his director, was the building and furnishing of the palace of Versailles. There the Louis XIV style was established. The decorative arts of France then swung into their full stride.

Above all else the Louis XIV style is that of a King, a court, a royal workshop. Pomp, opulence, magnificence—but genuine, never merely bombastic—were its dominant characteristics. It was formal, symmetrical and richly decorated. Form and direction were rectangular as evidenced by high-back chairs, high cabinets, console tables that stood below tall mirrors. The ornament was large in scale. The patterns of the fabrics were bold; their color, rich and brilliant. War trophies, the acanthus leaf, and the sunburst were favored motifs.

Oak, walnut and chestnut were the woods most frequently employed, but many new kinds of finishes were used on them—lacquer, gilding, inlay, and metal mounts were added abundantly.

One of the chief craftsmen of this period was André Charles Boulle, whose furniture was ornamented with an intricate overlay of tortoise-shell, ebony, copper and tin. But while Boulle's popular fame rests upon this invention, it should be remembered that during his long career (he continued to work with his four sons until he was more than eighty) he also originated, changed and improved many forms. Due largely to Boulle's influence the massive, cumbrous, archaic chest became the practical, graceful chest-of-three-drawers. He freed tables of the useless, heavy, cross-piece between the legs. He invented the flat-top writing desk with the center free to receive the knees and with convenient drawers at either side.

A unique innovation of the Louis XIV period, and one which continues to influence French interiors to this day, was the rising popularity of Chinese ceramics, textiles and lacquer. The French were not yet seamen nor traders but their currency between 1660 and 1700 enjoyed much the same buying power and desirability as the American dollar does today. Therefore, the Dutch and Portuguese, who had established trading connections in the Orient, were eager to sell the wares they brought from the East to the prosperous and cultured French. The vogue for Chinese ceramics mounted to amazing proportions, not only by reason of their intrinsic beauty but because the making of porcelain was a secret known only to the Chinese. Louis XIV bought quantities of this "amazing" ware to decorate the rooms of his palaces. Members of his court followed suit and thus was brought about the union of Chinese and French decorative art which continues in vogue.

Rare genius and superb craftsmanship were expended in the creation of the Louis XIV style, but it did not endure. However, no consideration of French furnishings is complete without at least a brief study of it, for it is the keystone of the nation's decorative achievement. It established, for the first time, an appreciation of decorative art. It developed new forms which, though interpreted on much too lavish and grand a scale

Fig. 5 Louis XV Library in Miniature by Mrs. James Ward Thorne

for any homes other than palaces, served as a basis of structure and design for the Provincial craftsmen. It inspired the artist to create and the people to buy, and oddly enough they now began to have the money to do so.

Though France groaned under the weight of excessive taxes placed on her by the King and his finance minister, Colbert, a prosperous middle-class developed during this spectacular reign. Louis XIV permitted the nobility of his court to retain their lands, he taxed their fortunes; he allowed them freedom from responsibility, but his appointments were made among the bourgeoisie. Despite high taxes, prosperity developed among the middle-class. Capable and industrious business men laid the foundation for substantial fortunes. They spent this new-found money on their homes—just as Ameri-

14

Fig. 6 Louis XV Boudoir in Miniature by Mrs. James Ward Thorne

cans do today. Thus the ground was laid for the building and furnishing of the little homes of 18th Century France. The "rustique" and "regional"—decorative arts, stimulated by the ambition and methods of the Grand Monarch, inspired by his chosen craftsmen were destined to flower into the style which Americans term "French Provincial".

THE STYLE RÉGENCE (1715-1723)

This was the era of pleasure. To consider the 18th Century merely as an age of trivial frivolity is a gross injustice. It was the most brilliant creative epoch of France since the days when the Gothic cathedrals were built. Always France has produced great artists and talented craftsmen. She has never been completely without them,

15

though some decades have been more prolific than others. But this was the time when the genius of French craftsmen reached its most gracious accomplishment. During the 18th Century France became the capital of the world of culture—England, Germany, Sweden, Russia, even far off China and America turned to France for beauty. France was the leader of all nations.

Despite the heavy taxes resulting from the extravagant building and the unsuccessful foreign wars waged by Louis XIV at the turn of the 17th and 18th Centuries, a prosperous middle-class developed. The difference between noble and bourgeoisie was less defined. Decorative art was no longer the sole possession of an imperious King. Palaces gave place to homes. Magnificence yielded to grace and charm. The ardor was not for conquest but for pleasure. This new mood found expression in the style called Régence. And the people took their cue from the court.

The beginning of this 18th Century saw the great-grandson of Louis XIV, a lazy child, on the throne of France. The government passed into the hands of the Duc d' Orléans, nephew of the Grand Monarch and uncle of the child-king, Louis XV. The Regent and his court felt none of the compelling duty to the nation that had spurred their deceased sovereign. The pursuit of pleasure became the order of the day. This change was reflected in the decorative art of France with amazing clarity and emphasis.

Perhaps the most welcome feature of this new Régence style was its treatment of walls, ceilings, and furniture. The court had less money to spend. Therefore, the heavy gilding and ornate carving which characterized the style of Louis XIV was no longer possible, nor desirable. Regardless of the cause, the result was propitious. The ornamental motifs of mask and martial trophies were abandoned for charming arrangements of foliage and shell. Delicate traceries replaced the opulent carvings. Occasionally the wood was painted but never more than lightly gilded. Carving no longer filled every inch of the space. Air appeared. This did not indicate a lack of invention. The carver of the Régence was like the musician who knows the value of silence. The pause stimulated; it led the eye to new delights. There was nothing created more charming than the restrained wood-carvings called *boiseries,* that now appeared on the walls of the panelled rooms of the manors and of the court. And this new-found beauty did not rest here, it acted as an initiation to the Provincial craftsmen whose products were soon to fill the little homes of France.

The basic articles of furniture of the French home—wardrobe, table, chair and bed—were now interpreted in a multitude of variations. Tables were smaller and lighter, more delicately carved. Cabinets and chests became more graceful. Chairs assumed curved lines. The commode, the petite commode and the chaise-longue were invented. Beds and couches acquired new and more gracious forms.

The Régence was a brief period; it ushered in the style Louis XV which was to endure far beyond the time of that handsome, indolent King.

THE STYLE LOUIS XV (1715-1774)

Louis XIV spent money to glorify the state; the Regent for his pleasure. When Louis XV grew to manhood he was too lazy to spend. He showered his largess not on the simple, pious, retiring Polish Princess he married, Marie Leczinska, but on the mistresses he favored. Their expenditures drew the wonder and denunciation of the world. But there was one woman whose exquisite taste justified her extravagance.

While riding in the forest one day, Louis XV met a pretty girl, Mademoiselle Poisson. Born of the middle-class, she had married when very young a rich financier, Monsieur Lenormant d'Etoiles. The King, fascinated by her wit and beauty, soon made her Marchioness of Pompadour, and she reigned as the royal mistress until her death.

Intelligent and beautiful, the marquise was a woman of eclectic taste, keen ambition and untiring energy. The enormous sums that she received from the King were expended in the building and embellishment of her many homes. When she became enamored of porcelain, she conceived the idea of duplicating in France the manufactories of Saxony. The royal potteries of Vincennes and of Sèvres were founded by her. The King took them under his protection and the nobles, to insure royal favor, vied with one another in purchasing the output of these factories at fabulous prices. Furniture, textiles, metal-work, received scarcely less of the attention of the Marquise de Pompadour. Though the furnishings she ordered were intended for the court, the craftsmen of every province in France were stimulated to higher accomplishment by them. It was as if an electric current vitalized the talent of the nation. To individual genius was now added a new strength. The fundamental reason for the superb development of the Louis XV style was *unity*.

The characteristic of this asymmetrical style termed "rococo", was the *curve*.

The genius of Pierre Le Pautre was its source of inspiration. The style progressed to its maturity through the works of many gifted architects, sculptors, artists and ornamentalists among whom were Oppenorde, Vasse, Watteau, Boucher, Meissonnier and Pineau. They issued engravings and pattern books of their designs which served provincial craftsmen throughout the nation. The record of the interiors of homes may be seen in the etchings of Abraham Bosse, the paintings of Chardin, and the many prints and engravings published during the 18th and early 19th Centuries.

All materials, all design, entered into this conspiracy of charm. The legs of tables,

17

Fig. 7 Provincial Bedroom in Miniature by Mrs. James Ward Thorne. Middle 18th Century

chairs, beds, chests, the design of fabrics, the clay of porcelain and pottery, the metal of candlesticks, andirons, even pots, pans and the very carvings on the walls took up this theme . . . the rococo curve.

The line of the curve might be interrupted with a gay cadence of flowers, but the genius of the French craftsman continued it to its logical progression. It is never overburdened, always it is governed by that admirable quality that is typical of the French—understatement. Their free flights of fancy and fantasy were leagued with reason and order. There was liveliness, energy, spontaneity, but there was also a complete lack of self-consciousness. Their invention was so fertile that it harbored no mannerisms. It bubbled forth as artless and joyous as the laugh of a child.

The French craftsman now knew the inherent possibilities and limitations of his materials. Proportion and construction were no longer problems. He had a natural

18

talent for unity. He had mastered function. Even today one is amazed at the strength and comfort of his most delicate chairs. But to the craftsman of the early 18th Century, function was not enough. The purpose of his genius was beyond function—it was beauty. He set about to embellish his materials with a soul that sang.

Now all the woods of the provinces contributed their riches to the craftsman. Transportation was a problem, so the Provincial cabinet-maker was still confined to the woods of his own locality but his invention triumphed over monotony. He was already familiar with the mellow beauty of oak which was so responsive to his carving tools, but furniture now came to be made of chestnut and walnut, of cherry, bright and glowing. The light lustre of pearwood and applewood, the dark sheen of beech and ash, lent their charms to the new designs. Beeswax and elbow grease, plus the benediction of time, enhanced the natural beauty of these woods. While brown was the dominant color-tone of these woods, it ranged from almost-black to a sunny taffy shade.

Upholstery now came into use. Fabrics echoed the new mood of gaiety. Their colors were bright, fresh and clear. Naturalistic flowers bloomed on them in profuse effulgence. The motifs were large, generous—it was an expansive age. Ceramics, metals, wood—a myriad of decorative ornaments were plentifully produced and found their way into cottages and manors throughout France.

Fig. 8 Bathroom and Boudoir in Miniature by Mrs. James Ward Thorne. Period of the Revolution

THE STYLE LOUIS XVI (1774-1793)

A new mood took possession of France during the second half of the 18th Century. The days of play had passed. The economy of the country was out of joint. Life had become a serious business. Reality had to be met and it presented a stern face. Rumblings of discontent were heard everywhere, not loud, as yet, but deep and persistent. A revolution was in the making. When "The King Is Dead" was announced in 1774, the young Louis XVI, barely twenty, and his beautiful child-wife, Marie Antoinette, fell on their knees and prayed, "O God protect us, direct us, we are too young!"

Even before the death of the old King, the decorative arts had abandoned their volatile, superficial graces and had passed on to a more severe school. As if conscious of the volcano upon which the nation rested, and which was destined soon to erupt, the creative genius of its craftsmen turned to a study of the classic which possessed the reassuring quality of immortality.

About this time came the news of the successful excavations and researches at Herculaneum and Pompeii. The rediscovery of the classic beauties in these cities, which for many years had lain buried under the lava of Vesuvius, had a telling effect upon creative thought and influenced both the fine and decorative arts.

This new seriousness motivated the cabinet-makers in every village and hamlet throughout France. Now intellect assumed command. Their tools no longer played over their woods as spontaneously as children skip along a garden path. They moved with serious purpose, with dignity, with restraint.

Almost overnight the restless rococo *curve* became disciplined to the *straight line*. The cabriole leg gave place to one that was straight, sometimes fluted. Moldings were refined and no longer interrupted with spontaneous cadences of flowers, but with a trim rosette. The frames of chairs and sofas were reduced in size and were extended upward from the legs in one continuous line. Underbracing was discontinued for it argued against delicacy. The broad-seated bergère, devised to harbor the bouffant skirts of the more luxurious earlier era, was slimmed to trimmer proportions. The architectural details of cabinets, commodes and tables followed this new refinement. When curves were employed they were invariably long and slender.

The dominant decorative motif was the rosette. Garlands, rope carvings, festoons of ribbons, flaming torches, baskets of flowers, lyres, musical instruments, doves and urns were also favored. A fluted column was often used. The metal mounts for keyhole and pulls were smaller and simpler.

Preference in woods also changed. Oak, elm and beech and all which presented a heavier texture and darker tone were abandoned because they did not give the desired effect of grace and lightness. The new classic style was interpreted in walnut, fruitwoods, and acajou (mahogany). Their surfaces were more highly polished and frequently painted in soft greys, greens and blues. Marquetry, in designs of bouquets and musical instruments, ornamented the more sophisticated pieces. Always vigor gave place to charm.

Textiles followed the trend. Lighter colors were in vogue. Designs were small and dainty. An important innovation was the increased use of printed cottons, called percale, and toile. Decorative accessories were smaller, simpler in design—their forms, classic.

Fashions change more often where communities are peaceful and prosperous. But the stalwart Bretons still faced the challenge of the sea; the mountain-folk still wrestled against relentless weather; the gay Provençals, far from the ominous rumblings of the capital, still basked in their glorious sunshine and enjoyed the plenty of their fertile fields. It is not, then, surprising that the taste and desires of the people in these districts did not conform readily to the new classic pattern. The production of furniture in the Louis XVI style was chiefly confined to the provinces near Paris. About the only recognition of the new style in Brittany, Alsace, Provence and the Pyrenees, was a refinement of structure, and the application of Louis XVI motifs upon the curved Louis XV frames.

THE STYLE DIRECTOIRE (1795-1799)

The Golden Age of French Decorative Art ended with the beheading of the King Louis XVI and Marie Antoinette in 1793. Then came the "Reign of Terror" when the country was swept by a bloody revolution which overthrew the aristocracy, sent thousands to the guillotine, and the nation's currency into chaos. When the turmoil subsided, the nation was ruled by a Board of three Directors. During these few years a neo-classic style of furnishing termed *Directoire* was developed. It was based on the style Louis XVI and retained its classical restraint.

THE STYLE EMPIRE (1804-1830)

Napoleon Bonaparte was crowned Emperor of France in 1804. Born in poverty on the primitive island of Corsica, Napoleon worked and starved his way through military school, and was lifted up from the ranks by genius, ambition and opportunity. Though he could place a crown on his head, he never acquired culture. And his court suddenly possessed of wealth, squandered it in tasteless display.

But Napoleon was shrewd. He realized that though he had placed France on a

Fig. 9 Empire Drawing Room in Miniature by Mrs. James Ward Thorne

pinnacle of military power, the victories of war are soon forgotten. Martial fame is the most ephemeral of all. Napoleon knew that the French demanded of their sovereign more than a stable economy, and the doubtful conquest of far lands. Realists though they were, there burned in the hearts of all Frenchmen a transcendant love of beauty. They looked to their sovereign to inspire its realization.

Soon after Napoleon's coronation in the Cathedral of Notre Dame in Paris (December 2, 1804) he followed the plan put into effect so gloriously by Louis XIV. The Emperor summoned the artists and craftsmen of his land and ordered them to create a new type of decorative art. The result was the style called "Empire".

Napoleon's early campaigns had taken him to Rome and Egypt. He was obsessed with the idea of the glory and the power of the Caesars. Refinement and restraint seemed effeminate and weak to this militaristic monarch. He was determined that the achievements of the kings who had lived during the past two hundred years must be discarded—their greatness was too close. And the craftsmen pandered to his whim.

22

The result was the *Empire* style which is less French than any that has come out of that country. It was forced, artificial, insincere and hollow—as imitation invariably is. It made use of ancient forms but then proceeded to embellish them with a rash of martial and classical motifs.

Mahogany was the favored wood at the court of the Emperor. But mahogany polished to a sparkling gloss, the natural deep-toned lustre of the wood itself was forgotten. Surfaces were usually plain, occasionally they were painted and lightly gilded. Moldings were heavy and imposing. The frames were thick, the proportions cumbersome. Lines were straight, and when infrequently employed, the curves were bold and heavy. The legs were straight, turned and sometimes slightly curved. The feet were square or ended in a heavy claw. Supports were columns or scrolls and the mounts were of brilliant metal.

The motifs of the Empire style were masterpieces of Napoleonic flattery. They repeated symbolic designs from the lands of his conquests. The sphinx, winged griffin, lion, eagle; the cornucopia, sword, shield, laurel wreath, acanthus leaf; the Greek fret and caryatid were applied to the plain surfaces of the wood in great profusion. To these were added the star, representing the Emperor, his initial *N,* and the well-known Napoleonic bee, symbol of the productivity of his reign.

The most amazing fact is that out of this hodge-podge and forced effort, the genius of the provincial French craftsman did achieve beauty. When he kept the forms free from the measles of Napoleonic motifs, they stand clear and crisp. Their lines, when refined by his genius, have a pure, rhythmic beauty. Though they are never spontaneous and gracious, they do present fine drama. Not only mahogany but fruit-woods of light taffy color were frequently employed, and lacquer was popular.

The designs of fabrics and ornaments repeated the favored Napoleonic motifs. They are always formal, set, but they frequently have fine style. The colors of this period were strong emerald-green, bold yellow, brilliant sapphire-blue and chalk-white. In recognition of the Emperor's conquests, broad stripes reminiscent of the military tent were popular. The times were dramatic—did not a poor soldier boy become Emperor? And the furnishings of the period echo the strident note of the bugle.

At this time the bond between France and America was very close. France sold to us the territory of Louisiana. The Empire style came overseas quickly and actually enjoyed more followers among American craftsmen—notably Duncan Phyfe—than in France, its native land. For, save in the provinces near to Paris, little was produced. It seemed that with the death of her Kings, the creative urge of the French craftsman passed. He bequeathed a glorious heritage.

CHRONOLOGY OF FURNITURE STYLES

SOVEREIGN	DATE	WOOD	CONSTRUCTION	MOTIFS	UPHOLSTERY
HENRY IV	1589-1610	Walnut Oak	Square lines. Massive. Deep, heavy carving.	Geometric. Figures. Busts.	Almost none.
LOUIS XIII	1610-1643	Walnut Oak	Straight & curved. Knobbed & turned legs. Spirals applied as ornaments.	Geometric.	Leather. Wool. Homespuns. Needlework.
LOUIS XIV	1643-1715	Oak Walnut Lacquer Gilding	Straight. High. Massive. Formal. Elaborate carving. Curved stretchers.	Mask. Martial trophies. Sunburst. Acanthus.	As above. Damask. Moquette. Brocatelle. Velvet.
RÉGENCE	1715-1723	Oak Walnut	Rectangular & curved. Refined carving. Many innovations in forms.	Shell. Mask. Foliage. Acanthus.	Damask. Bourette. Silk. Wool. Linen.
LOUIS XV	1715-1774	Oak Walnut Fruitwoods	Curved line. Graceful. Cabriole leg, scroll foot. Bombé and serpentine front.	Flowers. Bouquets. Baskets. Musical instruments. Acanthus.	Bourette. Silk. Brocades. Chintz. Toile de Jouy.
LOUIS XVI	1774-1793	Mahogany Walnut Fruitwoods Lacquer	Straight line. Small scale. Legs straight, fluted, vase shaped. Light, restrained carving.	Urn. Birds. Lyre. Oak leaves. Rosette. Garden implements.	As above.
DIRECTORATE	1795-1799	As above	Similar to above.	As above.	As above.
NAPOLEON I	1799-1814	As above	Straight & curved lines. Proportions heavy, cumbersome. Bun and claw foot.	Palmetto. Laurel. Bee. Star. Cornucopia. Pineapple. Swan. Caryatid. Columns.	As above. Velvet. Satin.

24

*F*urniture

HE Frenchman is essentially a realist. When he set about to furnish a home, his first creative impulse was concentrated on the articles he deemed most essential. They were a chest or cupboard in which to store his precious possessions, then a bed and finally tables and chairs.

These basic pieces of furniture were used in all parts of France. For north or south, east or west, the French lived in much the same fashion. Their habits being similar, the architecture and the furnishings of their homes were the same. However, due to the slight variance in climate, temperament, and in a minor way to dress, furniture was adapted to the climatic conditions of the provinces in which it was made.

A study of the furniture made in the different parts of France discovers how it followed the national styles and yet was adapted to the provincial characteristics of the people by whom it was used. Perhaps the most pronounced divergence in type existed between two neighboring provinces—Brittany and Normandy.

Brittany corresponds to America's New England. A rockbound coast where farms must be persuaded to produce. The Bretons were a sturdy, austere, sea-faring people. There were few rich bourgeoisie among them. The line between rich and poor, noble and peasant, was strongly defined.

The Bretons favored the turner's technique, their furniture was sturdy, rustic, ornamented with many balusters and spindles, which were sometimes made of box-wood. Oak long remained their favorite wood, though chestnut and pearwood were sometimes used. Cherry appeared only in their finer pieces. The carving was shallow, the designs continued to be the diamond, Maltese cross, the circular disc, and the door panels were framed with uniform moldings, long after other provinces had adopted the rococo curve.

Normandy, neighbor of Brittany, might be compared to our Eastern seaboard—to Virginia and the Carolinas. The people were gayer, richer, but less self-sufficient, more susceptible to outside influence, more easily persuaded to accept the new. The furniture of Normandy became famous for its beautiful proportion, fine unity of design, and its charming detail. Laurel leaves, sprays of roses, entwined hearts, baskets and bouquets of flowers, were delicately carved over the surface of the wood.

In the mountainous regions of Southern France, and in the Basque country, the furniture made by the craftsmen continued to hark back to the type preferred in the times of their favorite Kings, Louis XIII and Henry IV, even when it was made many decades later. It has a strong, primitive beauty that endears it to many. In Alsace, Burgundy and Lyonnais, the taste was for the massive; in the middle provinces it tended toward the simple and gracious. In the districts that neighbor the province called the "Ile de France", of which Paris is the center, the furniture shows the influence of the court and had much the same gay feeling as that of Normandy, while in southern France—Provénce—there was more diversity of type and form, more individual expression on the part of the craftsmen. The robust, architectural frame had rich and varied ornamentation, but this was always tastefully subordinated to the architecture itself. The moldings were clear-cut and positive. The carving was delicate, shallow, almost profuse—olive branches, sheaves of wheat, grapes, were popular features of the wood-carver's repertoire for they are native products of the soil.

The admirable quality of sincerity, the ability to perform a function and at the same time to achieve spontaneous beauty, is the most endearing feature of French Provincial furniture. It is the basic reason why the products of the craftsmen of Old France continue, centuries later, to be delightful to live with in contemporary homes.

A simple method of determining the *style* of furniture is to observe the leg. It proceeds from the knobbed and spiral form of the Louis XIII period to the leg with S-shaped stretcher that appeared during the time of Louis XIV. The stretcher was abandoned during the Regency and the leg became curved (called cabriole) with the arrival of the style Louis XV. Toward the end of the long reign of this King a classic influence asserted itself and the period of Louis XVI saw the leg straight and fluted. Later a vase-shaped leg was also prevalent and was continued through the brief Directoire period. The Empire style brought about a decided change. The claw and bun were used as a support.

In addition to these structural indications of period style there is another feature of French Provincial furniture which deserves careful study and observation—*ornament.* Antiquaires eager to determine the date of a piece invariably give close scrutiny to its ornament. There are four ornamental motifs that repeatedly appear in the decorative arts of Old France. They are the cartouche and the acanthus leaf, the mask and the trophy. They are shown on pages 30-31.

The development of French ornament was not confined to the efforts of cabinet-maker, weaver and smithy. There was a group of artists, who were known as "ornamentalists", a term similar to but more comprehensive than the contemporary name "designers". Many of these men never had a tool in their hands and therefore were not craftsmen. Many of them were distinguished engravers, etchers and draughtsmen. Thus they served as an important link between the fine arts and the decorative arts and the trades. Books of engravings presenting the designs of the ornamentalists were published and gained wide distribution. These books served as newspapers to the trades. They educated the taste of the public, spurred it to acquisition; inspired and instructed the craftsmen in the designs of the period. The contents of these books were sometimes original but oftentimes stemmed from the fine arts or were the ornamental designs of painters, sculptors and architects. For it must be remembered that from the time of Louis XIV the fine and decorative arts were intimately united. Artists and sculptors did not limit their creative genius to canvas and marble. They also worked in textiles, ceramics, metals and wood. They created entire rooms, from the pictures mounted in the panelling to the key that opened the door.

The fine arts of France between the 17th and 19th Centuries describe a circle. The painters of the time of Louis XIV sought their inspiration from Italy and Rome. The figures in the paintings of Le Brun and his contemporaries are not men and women. They are Muses and Gods. A study of the classics and of mythology was the order of the day and they were the source of the artists' inspiration. This art was harmonious with the spirit of the times for it was created to serve as a setting for a King who declared "I am the State" and for a nation that aspired to the cultural supremacy of the world. The spirit of order, formality, and discipline was dominant.

But with the passing of Louis XIV and the coming of the Duc d' Orléans as Regent, an emotional revolution occurred. The shackles of discipline were broken. The portraits of Mignard express this change, for in them you see vital, live women; they do not float in clouds but sit in luxurious chairs. The vogue for pleasure is evidenced by the frequency with which the chosen scene was the theatre, fete and carnival. Watteau is the prime painter of this epoch. A national spirit was manifested by an increasing delineation of the countryside, its little sunlit streams, its silvery-leafed trees, its mirror lakes and sequestered bowers. But whatever the locale of a picture might be, it was always a paradise.

This presentation of gaiety, of happiness, of delight, was followed by an art that emphasized freedom and acquisition. The paintings of the mid-18th Century are characterized by highly individualized technique and they are filled with furniture, objets d'art, and all the accoutrements of luxurious living; the men and women depicted in them are magnificently dressed. The spirit of the rococo reached its full expression through the genius and skill of the brushes and pigments of Boucher and Fragonard.

Simultaneously the bourgeoisie was entering upon its social maturity. It had become aware of its inherent rights and riches. The individual had acquired self-respect. A full life for people as well as for kings dawned; it was of necessity more simple, but it could be gracious. Chardin painted the "little people" of France with equal genius and with the attention that once had been accorded to Gods and Kings.

Then art itself became democratic. The paintings of the Masters were engraved and prints were widely dispersed. A medium developed to a high degree was the use of red chalk termed "sanguine", which introduced color that could be worthily and inexpensively reproduced. Pictures were no longer confined to palaces; they entered the home and books illustrated with engravings were popular.

The next scene to be recorded was the "joys of the simple life". The locale of paintings moved from Olympus and Paradise, from theatre and salon, to the garden and countryside. The Goncourts, unexcelled commentators on 18th Century France, declared that it was, "The most essentially French century in our national history".

Then came the Revolution, the Directorate, and as the 19th Century dawned, Napoleon. Art, led by the whims of the Emperor, and the paintings of David, returned to Olympus and to Rome. Within a century and a half, a complete circle had been described.

The artists who worked through these centuries not only made an important contribution to fine art, their pictures also serve as invaluable documents on the decorative arts of France. There is no more illuminating commentary nor more instructive data to be found than the paintings, etchings and engravings of these times. In them you may see the structure and ornament of furnishings, how mirrors were placed, furniture upholstered, and draperies hung, even to a tassel. As a preliminary reading guide to this rich source material the following chart is offered. The listing is not definitive and it must be remembered that the work of artists and ornamentalists was never strictly confined within the limits of the reign which lent its name to the style.

CHART OF STYLES, ARTISTS AND ORNAMENTALISTS

STYLE LOUIS XIII

ARTISTS

Poussin	Félibien	Puguet
Claude Lorraine	van der Meulen	Desjardins
Le Sueur	de Berthelot	Coyzevox
Bosse	Anguier	Callot
Bourdoin	Guillan	
de Champagne	Girandon	

ORNAMENTALISTS

Barbet	Toutin
Vouet	Hurtu
Boyvin	L'Égaré
Biard	Moncornet
Vovert	Caillard
Morien	Le Febvre

STYLE LOUIS XIV

ARTISTS

Le Brun	Le Largillière
Mignard	Picart
Le Moyne	Benoist
Gillot	Nanteuil

ORNAMENTALISTS

Loir	Marot
D'Avilier	Boulle
Jean Le Pautre	Francart
Pierre Le Pautre	Mansart
Berain	Le Clerc

STYLE RÉGENCE

Watteau	Raoux	Pineau	Cressent
Oudry	Rigaud	La Joue	Audran
Coypel	Appenard	Le Roux	Abbadies

STYLE LOUIS XV

ARTISTS

Boucher	Nattier	Drouais	Tocqué
Fragonard	Natoire	Dumont	Tournières
Chardin	Eissen	De La Tour	Trèmollière
Pigalle	Saint-Aubin	Perronneau	
Lancret	Aved	Pesne	
Pater	Desportes	Robert	

ORNAMENTALISTS

Meissonnier	de Cuvilliès
Babel	Bourchardon
Gravelotte	Le Prince
Meil	Chamblin
Blondel	Oppenord
Briseux	Pillement

STYLE LOUIS XVI

ARTISTS

Vigée-Lebrun	Moreau
Lavrience	Huet
Greuze	Vien
Cochin	Vernet
Nilson	Le Moine

ORNAMENTALISTS

Ranson	Lalonde
Roubo	Desprez
Berthault	Salembier
de la Rottiére	De La Fosse
de Wailly	

STYLE EMPIRE

ARTISTS

David
Prud'hon

ORNAMENTALISTS

Fay
Percier
Normond
Fontaine

Louis XIII

Louis XIV

Louis XV

Louis XVI

Empire

Louis XIII

Louis XIV

Louis XV

Louis XVI

Empire

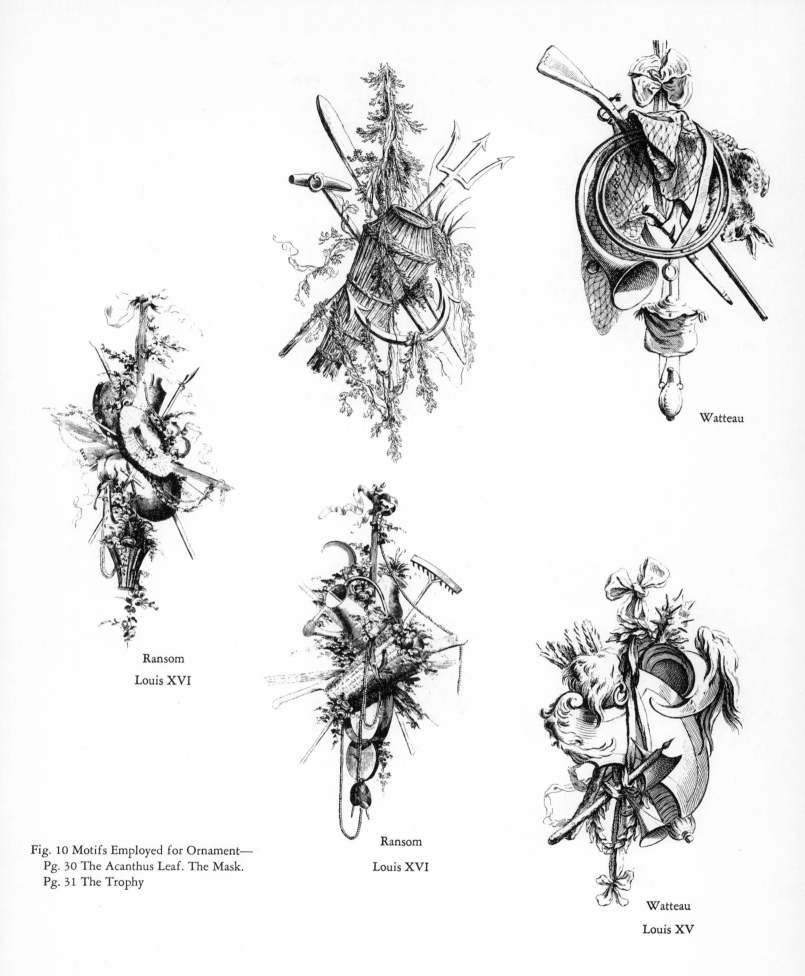

Watteau

Ransom
Louis XVI

Fig. 10 Motifs Employed for Ornament—
Pg. 30 The Acanthus Leaf. The Mask.
Pg. 31 The Trophy

Ransom
Louis XVI

Watteau
Louis XV

31

Fig. 11 Ornament in the Style of Louis XV

Ransom

Fig. 12 Ornament in the Style of Louis XVI

Salambier

Fay

Fig. 13 Ornament in the Style of the Empire

CHAPTER IV

Armoires and Cupboards

T HE dominant feature of the French Provincial home was a large cupboard called "Armoire". Its purpose was to hold the family's possessions—clothes, linens, silver, dinnerware, even food. It was built on a robust, architectural frame and stood on low legs. There were two styles of construction: one which had long double doors extending from top to base. The other—called the "armoire de deux corps"—was built in two stories, with the lower portion decidedly larger than the top one. This type had double doors on each section.

The first *armoires* were made in France during the later years of the 17th Century and clearly show the influence of the lands from which their inspiration came—Italy, Germany, Flanders and Spain. Marquetry, ebony, tooled leather, ivory and even semi-precious stones, ornamented the cupboards imported from these lands for the kings and their courts. German importations showed the use of paint, with stylized flowers and bouquets painted on the doors. Though the French provincial craftsmen accepted the basic design originated by their foreign confréres, they soon developed their own style and brought the *armoire* to its zenith during the reign of Louis XV.

Oak was the wood preferred for this important piece of furniture, though walnut and chestnut were sometimes used. Along the coast, where it was possible to obtain exotic woods from the ships that put into port, ebony and mahogany were cut into moldings and applied as ornament. Paint was employed by the craftsmen along the northern border and their embellishments and massive structures evince a strong Germanic influence.

During the 18th Century fruitwood came into favor, especially in southern and in central France, and it remained in vogue until the end of the century when the Empire mode favored mahogany.

French *armoires* show four distinct styles. Those made in the time of Henry IV and Louis XIII are nearly square and made in one or two stories. They have deep cut moldings, sometimes a spiral column on the ends and between the doors. The doors are divided by heavy moldings into deep square panels. These are vigorously carved in bold, geometric designs such as circles, diamond-point stars, the Maltese cross and the diamond itself. The dark, lustrous surface ornamented with simple, deep moldings and proud, bold carvings, never overdone, yet frankly and completely expressed, created a rich, impressive simplicity. These *armoires* have splendid proportions, a unity of design and frank virility that express the superior skill and fine taste of the French cabinet-maker.

After the turn of the 17th Century the massive lines of the *armoire* were refined. The swelled bombé front and in-curved doors appear. The moldings are lighter and follow the rococo curve. The door-panels have a typical S-shape. The whole effect is one of height rather than of breadth. The solid, massive appearance gives place to one of grace. The severe geometric carvings on the panels are relinquished for graceful sheaves of wheat, olive branches, grapes and flowers.

In Normandy the *armoire* acquired a "fronton"—an ornamental board or bonnet which extended across the top. It was sometimes scalloped and supported by round and fluted columns. Often it was beautifully carved with bouquets or baskets of flowers. These carvings were shallow, delicate, almost profuse.

Doors were ornamented with long hinges and lock escutcheons made of brass or steel were elaborately chased with harmonious designs. These metal ornaments bring a delightful sparkle to the deep tones of the wood and are charming bits of beauty that bespeak the skill of the metal worker. Even the keys have distinction. Their frets are wrought in intricate lace-like designs but they have withal an honest sturdiness.

The *armoire* reached its zenith during this period (the early 18th Century) and never quite lost the important mein it assumed at this time. As the years passed it adapted itself to the classic style of Louis XVI merely by changing its moldings from the curve to the straight line. The carvings became more restrained and motifs of ribbons and musical instruments were added to the wood-carver's repertoire. The *armoire* of the Louis XV period had a definite style, while those that followed immediately after were really transition pieces.

A decided change came in with the Empire. Acajou—as the French term mahogany—was the wood most in use. The pieces are smaller and more shallow. The doors show no carving; the wood is highly polished. The elongated hinges and escutcheons are abandoned. In their place appear bands of intricately chased bronze. These are applied to the top and bottom of the half-round columns which run from base to bonnet on either side of the frame. When these columns are broken at top and base by a square it is often ornamented with a bronze star or rosette. The low legs, which once followed the line of the frame so much as to seem not legs but a part of the structure, disappear and a massive bun or carved claw forms the support.

Comparatively few *armoires* were made in this period. Far into the 19th Century this piece of furniture remained true to the style of the favorite kings of the separate districts. In Northern France and in Brittany, the stalwart, rustic style of the earlier periods prevailed, and painted pieces reflecting Germanic influences continued to be preferred in the northeast. In southwest France and along the Atlantic coast the cupboards in the styles of Henry IV and Louis XIII prevailed while Provénce and central France remained true to the rococo curve and Normandy to its light flower carvings and elaborate fronton.

The *armoire* gave birth to a cupboard which was given the appropriate name "bonnetiére". In many of the provinces of France, especially in Brittany and Normandy, the women wore bonnets which were marvels of lace, linen and frills. Also, one might add, of laundering. These bonnets were worn on special occasions and between times were carefully stored away. This custom created the need for a piece of furniture in which to store the headgear of the women of the family.

The *armoire* usually measured about six feet wide, seven feet high and about two feet deep. The *bonnetiére* was narrower, shallower, shorter and had but one door. Shelves were placed in it and on them the fanciful millinery rested. These cupboards have the same type of molding and carved ornament as their parent piece and were originally placed along the wall side by side with the larger pieces. As the family possessions increased with its prosperity, more cabinets were acquired until it was not unusual to see an entire wall panelled with cupboards of varying widths and heights. Thus 18th Century France conceived "built-in" furniture now considered modern.

Fig. 14 Louis XIV Corner Cupboard of
Black Lacquer with Chinoiserie Design

Fig. 15 Louis XV Oak Cupboard with
Rococo Carving

Figs. 16, 17 Régence Oak Cupboards

Fig. 16

Fig. 17

39

Fig. 18 Louis XV Two-door Cupboard

Fig. 19 Louis XV Fruitwood Cupboard
in Two Parts

Fig. 21 Rustic Cupboard of Oak from
Brittany. Circa 1807

Fig. 20 Oak Cupboard in Two Parts
Showing Stylized Carving and Straight
Moldings. Late 18th Century

41

Escutcheons and Keyholes for Cupboards

Fig. 22 Louis XVI Fruitwood Bookcase.

42

CHAPTER V

Beds

N the early years of the 17th Century when the French bourgeoisie and farmers began to furnish their homes, the bed was literally hewn out of oak. It consisted of four upright posts from which serge curtains were suspended to keep out cold, dampness and draughts.

As the decades passed, this functional bed began to adjust itself to the climate of the province in which it stood. In the southern parts of the country where the climate was mild, even warm, the lower bed-posts gradually disappeared until only a foot-board was used. The bed was placed against one wall of the room with decorative hangings suspended from its two tall headposts, or if they too had disappeared, the draperies were merely attached to the wall on a frame and extended as a canopy over the top of the bed.

Cold weather prevails in the mountainous parts of France and along the northwest seacoast. There the bed was built into the walls. Even the protection of hangings was not sufficient to keep out the elements and doors with upper-panels pierced with spindles were substituted. These actually made of the bed a closet. In Brittany, the land of the seafarers, these built-in beds were placed one on top of the other. The long side faced the wall, and across it stood a chest with a double purpose. It served as a mount when getting into bed and also as storage space for garments and quilts.

43

As the homes of France began to be built more solidly and therefore afforded better protection from the weather, the bed lost its protective features and gradually assumed a decorative as well as a functional purpose.

First the posts at the foot disappeared. This gave an impetus towards importance for the head-board. During the time of Louis XIV it became very high, rising four to even six feet, and ending with a decorative scalloped edge. Gradually this was reduced and head and foot-boards became almost the same height. The bed-ends were rounded in deep bulging swells, like a sleigh. In the country houses of the wealthy, these frames were heavily padded and upholstered with fabrics. A spread of the same material as the upholstery was used. The side rails were profusely carved with flowers and vines.

The beds in less prosperous homes followed the same lines. The moldings were deep, and followed the rococo curve. The surface of the wood of the panels at head and foot was elaborately carved with characteristic motifs—flowers, leaves, baskets, bouquets and bowknots. They had cabriole legs often traced with the acanthus leaf.

When the rococo style gave place to the classic, straight line (Louis XVI) the frames of the beds followed suit. Both head and footboards became flat, straight and slender. The carving on the panels was abandoned and the skill of the designer found expression only in the moldings. These were delicately carved in rope designs, the egg and dart pattern, and served to frame the plain panels. The legs became straight, squat and fluted. Sometimes the panels of the foot and head-boards between the carved moldings were upholstered. This upholstery had a characteristic method of application.

During the Louis XV period the padding beneath the upholstery raised it from the frame of the panel in a soft, rounded bulge. During the Louis XVI period, the upholstery was *boxed*—that is, it came out sharply and squarely from the panel for about two inches. This sharp line was emphasized by a cording or guimpe, and then the fabric descended smoothly along the flat surface of the frame.

With the advent of the Directoire and Empire styles the frame of the bed experienced another decided change. The foot-board rose to the same height as the head-board. The moldings were extremely simple though deeper. On them typical motifs of the period were lightly carved—the urn, rosette, laurel-leaf.

Painted furniture came into vogue during the last quarter of the 18th Century so that many beds of this later period are painted in bone-white, oyster-grey and sometimes robin's-egg blue and mint-green. Often the moldings are lined with a darker color in contrast to the panels.

The style again changed with the advance of the 19th Century. Beds came to be made of mahogany cut in heavy, massive lines. They rested on broad, square feet or claws. They were ornamented with rosettes and sometimes with swags of stylized laurel leaves molded of bronze. However, these massive beds of mahogany favored by Napoleon and his satellites are seldom found outside the area of Paris and cannot be considered truly Provincial.

A charming feature of the beds of France was their coverings and draperies. The dreary serge curtains of the frugal days of Henry IV and Louis XIII would not long satisfy the Frenchwoman's love of gaiety. Her long winter evenings were spent weaving linen. This was embellished with charming designs embroidered in bright colored threads of wool and silk. Not only the spread but valances and curtains were produced by her industrious and accomplished needle.

When the power-looms were invented in the early 19th Century and cloth became less costly and more readily available, the new opportunity to embellish the home which resulted was eagerly seized. Layers of cotton were laboriously quilted between the gay printed toiles, chintz and percales, and thus were created warm and sturdy quilts whose designs are silent but eloquent arguments for French skill and taste.

After the introduction of toiles and figured chintzes the hangings of the bed were merely decorated with fringe and guimpe, while the same material was lined with cotton and quilted to serve as a warm covering on the bed. This same fabric was also used to upholster the head and foot-boards. Often these decorative fittings eclipsed in beauty the bed itself.

Fig. 23 Louis XV Bed of Fruitwood

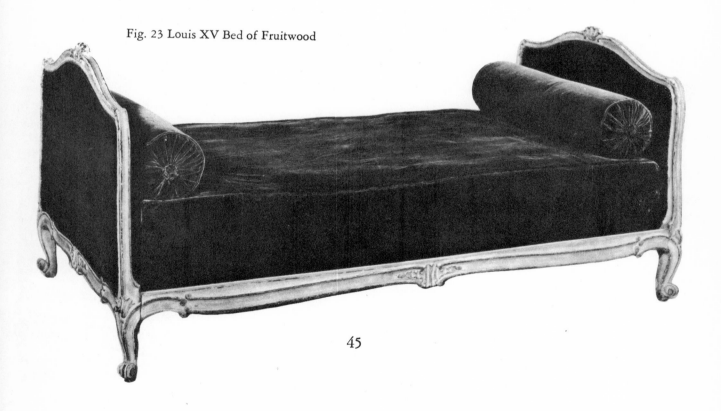

Fig. 24 Four-poster Bed with Chintz
Hangings. Late 18th Century

Fig. 25 Louis XVI Painted Bed

46

Fig. 26 Empire Painted and Gilded Bed

Fig. 27 Louis XVI Painted Bed

Fig. 28 Louis XV Bed-wall with Cabinets

CHAPTER VI

Buffets

RANCE is the land of the gourmet. It is also the nation of the buffet. For among women who take pride in their cooking it is predestined that the accoutrements for serving food take a place of recognized importance in their home.

Even as early as the days of Louis XIII the buffet made its appearance but its full development did not occur until the beginning of the 18th Century. In size, shape and structure it closely resembled the *armoire*. It had the same architectural lines, rich moldings, charming carvings, and was constructed in both one and two sections.

The buffet was usually made with two or three drawers over the bottom part which had two or three doors. The upper section, more shallow than the lower, consisted of a series of open shelves, small cupboards, and might even provide a niche for a statue of the Virgin. Most impressive of all, and emphatically announcing the prosperity of the family, was the buffet which was topped by a clock!

All of these divertissements which occurred on the upper section, and they were myriad, were attached to a back-board and framed by moldings and a carved bonnet so that the piece presented a beautiful effect of unity and proportion.

Arranged on the open shelves were the eating and cooking utensils of the family. Sunlight and candlelight were caught and reflected by the generous quantity of gleaming copper and the dim lustre of pewter, which were one of the most delightful features of the French Provincial home. Kettles, jugs, pots, porringers, spoons and measures, ingenious in invention, delightful in shape and excellent in craftsmanship, sparkled on the shelves and lent gaiety to this utilitarian piece of furniture. Following them, as the century progressed, came beautiful ceramics which made of every buffet a brilliant flower garden. In the south of France and in the central sections where it is dry and dusty, the tall buffet was made with its shelves enclosed both top and bottom. French-women are meticulous housekeepers.

A smaller edition of the buffet was also popular. It was called a "bahut" and consisted of a long, narrow cupboard similar to the American sideboard. It had no open shelves and was made in two styles . . . with two or three doors below the board or with one or two shallow drawers immediately below the board and beneath them a compartment with double doors. On all of these pieces the legs were short, either cabriole or straight of line.

The large buffet with open shelves to harbor table and cooking wares was called "Buffet Vaisselier". A modification of its construction was the smaller piece called simply "Vaisselier". This stood on very low legs and consisted of a series of open shelves with an ornamental carved board extending across the front of each shelf or a board similarly placed in which spindles were inserted. These served as supports to keep the ware standing upright.

Another offshoot of the buffet was a piece called "garde mangé"—or food guard. This was a narrow cupboard with one long door extending from top to bottom. Into the panel of this door a metal grille or a series of spindles were inserted to permit the passage of air. The *garde-mangé* was constructed and ornamented with carvings, hinges and escutcheons in the same styles as the grand buffets.

Oak and walnut were the favorite woods when the cabinet-maker made a buffet. He continued to use these dark woods right into the 19th Century in the northern, western and southwestern sections of the country. But in Normandy, central and south-eastern France, fruitwoods of a beautiful warm, nut-brown color came into prominence. Cherry was sometimes used for the finer pieces, but the wood of the apple and pear maintained its popularity. The inherent beauty of these woods with their natural lustrous surface, polished by use and years, is a delight to the eye—there is no substitute for the beautiful patine of age.

Oak is a vigorous, sturdy wood, its stalwart aspect is ideally suited to the rustic interpretation of the buffet. The French Provincial cabinet-maker carved it into rich moldings, the panels of the doors had deeply incised designs of geometric and stylized motifs, while the open shelves were ornamented with many spindles.

50

When oak was used for the low buffet—the *bahut* or *buffet-bas* as the piece was termed—the moldings were pronounced, the carving little more than traceries of simple circles and stars, with primitive flowers, leaves or vines framing the doors.

The buffets made of the lighter fruitwoods have simple door panels with a firm, but not deep molding, repeating an S-shaped curve, the decorative grain and color of the wood serve as the sole source of decoration. But walnut, cherry and the rarer quality of fruitwoods inspired the carver to do his utmost. These are profusely carved with the favorite motifs of the native provinces—hearts, baskets of flowers, sprays of olive leaves. They flow gaily over door panels, and the bonnet, which was often supported by round or fluted columns.

Usually the age and native province of the buffet can be determined by the manner in which it is carved. The earlier ones of oak and walnut have the deep-cut stylized motifs characteristic of the Henry IV and Louis XIII periods. Pronounced moldings, outlined with a brief tracery and combined with foliage or shell, denote the Régence period. The simple S-shaped panels and also profuse carving, generally infer the Louis XV era. When the curve changes to the straight line and the carving becomes more restrained, the buffet is usually of the later 18th Century.

Hinges and locks are important features of the buffet. They are elongated more than seems necessary, but French Provincial furniture was made for generations of wear. Made of steel or brass, they are intricately designed, often elaborately chased, and they create a delightful contrast with the lustrous patine of the wood.

Very few bookcases are found among the products of the French Provincial craftsmen. The farmer had few books and probably less time and inclination to read them; then too, the French are a social people. Work in the fields was begun at dawn, finished only at dusk, when the meager light of candles and oil did not invite reading. With duties done, the gregarious French enjoyed company and they were never isolated on farms as were Americans, so evenings and Sundays were times for visiting between families and for meetings with friends at the café. For the French live in little clusters of cottages and go out to work their small farms a kilometer or so away; such extensive acreage as was known in America was beyond their ken.

The homes of the town-folk were often possessed of panelled walls which included sections for books. However, from these homes came the few bookcases of the early periods. The appearance of these bookcases is very similar to the more refined types of *armoire* and buffet made in the Louis XV style. The doors are infrequently glazed, usually their panels have a decorative wire grille and the frames are made of oak or walnut. They are almost never large pieces of furniture as was the English breakfront.

Their measurements are usually about five or six feet high and four feet wide.

The use of bookcases became more prevalent during the late 18th Century. These have strong, simple frames of fluted moldings of the Louis XVI style and are frequently painted in solid colors—bone-white, grey or black lacquer. Their doors are grilled.

During the Empire even more bookcases were produced. They are built of mahogany or of fruitwood with glazed doors and follow the straight lines typical of the period. The bonnet is supported by half-round columns which extend upward along the sides. The feet are a low bun, a claw, or they are straight and thick.

However, the lover of books and of French Provincial furnishings need not be put off his quest by the lack of specific furniture to house his books, even if his purse will not permit the purchase of a beautiful old panelled room with inset bookshelves. The spacious old *armoires,* buffets and cupboards simply "eat up" books. They easily store them at least two rows deep. However, sympathy is due the woman whose house was filled with fine books in beautiful old *armoires,* who said that her idea of Heaven was a place where books stood at hand's reach in single rows.

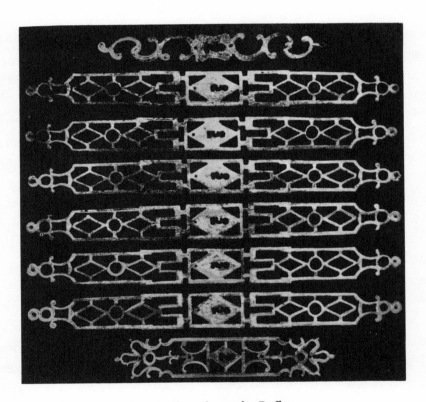

Fig. 29 Escutcheons for Buffets

Fig. 30 Fruitwood Buffet with Open Shelves and Fret-work Steel Escutcheons. 18th Century

Fig. 31 Louis XV Buffet with Doors in Two Parts

53

Fig. 32 Louis XV Low Buffet of Fruitwood with Two Drawers. Faïence Ornaments

Fig. 33 Louis XV Long Buffet of Oak with Light Surface Carvings

Fig. 34 Buffet of Cherry with Drawers for
Eating Utensils. Late 18th Century

Fig. 35 Louis XV Fruitwood Buffet

55

Fig. 36 Louis XVI Sideboard of Mahogany
with Marble Top and Brass Galleries

Fig. 37 Louis XVI Mahogany Buffet with
Drawers for Silver. Marble Top

CHAPTER VII

Chairs and Stools

F it were necessary to choose one piece of furniture in which the skill, the practicality, the wit, the taste, and the genius of the French Provincial cabinet-maker was most completely expressed, it would be the chair. From the squat four-square stools of Spain, and the sprawling peg-leg seats of Germany, the French craftsman developed the chair to the epitome of strength, comfort and beauty.

A French chair has as much character and personality as any person you may know. It may be sturdy and forthright; frivolous and chatty; dignified and formal; luxurious, graceful, dramatic, inventive, reserved, humorous . . . in a word, French chairs are *portraits*. They are all the people you know interpreted in wood and fabric far more clearly than the camera can record them. To assemble a collection of French chairs is to bring into being a litany of saints and sinners. Such an assembly would be delightful to possess and yet so fertile were those craftsmen of the provinces that if you purchased one hundred—two hundred chairs—there would always be another that you would wish to invite to join the party.

The first generation of French chairs were merely stools, four sticks down and a plank across. Quite obviously they were suggested by the stools of Spain and of Italy. During the days of Henry IV the Provincials learned to make seats with turned legs. Then a straight, upward back was added. Louis XIII saw the legs and the back frames turned into spirals, making the chair appear squat and square. Occasionally leather was added for seats and upholstery. But comfort was still unknown.

From Germany came the idea of a shaped seat and back attached to sprawling peg-legs. These remained popular in the border provinces for many decades.

In the reign of Louis XIV the vogue for chairs called for straight, high backs. These had the back and seat upholstered or perhaps only the seat, in serge, leather or homespuns. Nail-heads obviously marked the joining of fabric and wood. The legs were straight and ended in a scroll, between them was an S-shaped stretcher.

It was probably in Provénce that the most popular type of chair was first made— the "fauteuil de Capucine." Its vogue continues throughout the French countryside to this day.

This chair had a rush seat, a ladder-back and legs that were short, sturdy, usually straight but sometimes turned into knobs. It often had a valanced front which was charmingly carved. Eventually it acquired an arm and later, much later, a pad made of fabric quilted with cotton or wool, and finally a deep cushion of feathers was added to introduce comfort to the rush seat.

In Normandy, always more aware of the court than the other provinces, the rush-bottom chair was given an open back with a lyre carving—the lyre being a favorite Louis XVI motif.

Stools with rush seats and turned legs were favorite articles in French homes long after the chair came into casual use. Their frames followed the general lines of the chairs. In fact, the French have always made much use of stools, a custom that America would do well to copy.

In addition to chairs and stools with short turned legs, ladder-backs and rush seats, the French Provincial craftsmen also made a settee which was called a "canapé." In construction it was identical with the *fauteuil de Capucine,* but would seat two, three, sometimes four people. Its ladder-back repeated the curve of the chair frame and it was sometimes given a flat cushion of brilliant-colored quilted fabric. The *canapé,* along with the chairs, also acquired an open wooden arm. It usually stood near the fireplace, for stools and benches were used when dining at table.

At first, oak, beech, and ash only were employed in the making of chairs. These woods were left in their natural color or painted until along toward the end of the 17th Century when chairs were also made of walnut and fruitwood.

With the coming of the Régence there came a change in chairs. The lines heretofore had been straight and square. Now they were more rounded. They acquired cane back and seats. The frames were carved with rocaille ornament. The legs were slightly curved, frequently an acanthus leaf was carved on them. The chaise longue was popular at this time. In the homes of the prosperous, upholstery and cushions now were introduced, comfort and pleasure being the order of the day.

Women's dress had a great deal to do with the evolution of the chair. By the beginning of the 18th Century skirts had become enormous. The cabinet-maker provided for them by creating a chair with a broad seat and low arms. It permitted a lady to sit comfortably and spread her skirts so that the full effect of her costume might be admired. This chair was termed a "bergère". It was upholstered with heavy padding, covered with fabric. A loose cushion filled the seat.

This chair in the Louis XV period was broad and low. It stood on cabriole legs. Its frame curved sensuously and was handsomely carved, its lines were often broken by cadences of flowers at the top and along the front valance. The back was high, usually corset-shape, but only infrequently had wings.

Conversation was an art in these times and numerous chairs, easily movable, were necessary furnishings of a room. This need created the type of chair now termed "occasional". It was smaller in size than the *bergère,* but also was upholstered on seat and back. The arms were open and eventually acquired pads for arm-rests. Its frame followed the rounded lines typical of the period and it had a carved valance and the omnipresent cabriole leg. Sometimes the upholstery was abandoned and seat and back were caned, with a pad added for comfort.

The upholstery fabrics used on these chairs was of large design, naturalistic flowers being favored. The material might be needle-point (gros point preferred), velvet, wool, silk, linen or chintz, as budget and the mood of the room dictated.

The so-called straight chair of this period (Louis XV) is usually carved of walnut or beech. The frame flows in a curved line, sometimes broken with flowers and sometimes uninterrupted. Seats and backs are upholstered with fabric or caned, at which time a loose cushion is added.

A type of chair unique to France of this period is a straight-back chair with a very broad low seat, always comfortably upholstered. These are rare and costly, but when found, are delightful adjuncts to a room.

The dressing table of the wealthy woman was a flat table, painted or adorned with fabric or lace on which a low mirror stood. A chair was needed when making her toilette and the French craftsmen devised one of the most beautiful of seats. It was three-cornered. The frame was lightly carved and flowed rhythmically down from a high rounded back to low arms. The legs were cabriole. The apron was broad and fancifully carved with flowers. The broad, deep seat was fitted with a flat fabric pad.

Most of these chairs show evidence of grey, putty-color, or dull yellow paint. Obviously they were not made for farm cottages but for the manors of the wealthy.

When the gracious mood of the early 18th Century passed to the more serious one that marked its closing years, chairs followed the trend toward classic restraint. The types remained much the same—*bergère,* occasional chair, side chair, chaise longue —but the rounded line and curved leg disappeared.

Now the frames were lightly fluted along straight lines, the curving shapes became thinner, flatter. The cadences of flowers resolved themselves into a rosette. The legs were tapered, fluted and straight. Upholstery and cushions were slimmed and the fabrics which were employed were harmonious. Textiles with small flowers, tiny gay bowknots, meandering ribbons and slender stripes, were admirably suited to the refinement of the frames on which they were placed. The favorite materials are petit point (not gros point), taffeta, chintz and toiles. Small motifs are the rule.

When Napoleon became Emperor of the French the mode changed once again. The chairs and tables made in the Empire Style by the French Provincial craftsmen are unquestionably the most beautiful products of this period.

The side chairs of this Empire era are exceptionally lovely. The lines are fine, trim and crisp. The backs are high, sometimes they rise like a comb. Medallions of swans and charming little animals are carved in the center. In a set of chairs the carving of each back panel will be different. The legs are slender, sometimes turned into knobs, sometimes slightly curved with the back legs at variance with the front legs. This union of two kinds of legs on one chair can be a forced conceit, but oftentimes it creates a surprising effect of beauty. The valance was carved with an urn, laurel leaves or other typical Empire motifs.

The arm chairs are straight, severe to look upon, but amazingly comfortable. The frames have flat lines but are too often ornamented with swans, caryatids, and the legs sometimes end in a thick claw. When the lines are kept clear, the chairs of this late period are beautiful.

Fruitwood of a light, taffy color and mahogany, dark and lustrous, were employed in making the chairs of this period. Many of these later chairs were painted an oyster-grey or bone-white and the lacquer made an interesting contrast to the colorful mustard, emerald-green or sapphire-blue fabrics with which they were upholstered.

The chairs of the Empire period do not have the spontaneous, buoyant beauty of the Louis XV style, nor yet the classic simplicity of the style Louis XVI, but they have chic and contribute drama to the French Provincial interior.

Fig. 38

Fig. 39

Figs. 38, 39, 40, 41 Chairs of the Late 17th Century

Fig. 40

Fig. 41

61

Fig. 42 Louis XIV Armchair Upholstered in Tapestry

Fig. 43 Régence Armchair Upholstered in Tapestry with Carved Oak
Frame

Fig. 44 Louis XV Armchair with
Cane Back and Seat

Fig. 45 Louis XV Side Chair of
Walnut with Cane Seat and Back

Fig. 46 Louis XV Three-corner
Chair of Beechwood with Horse-
shoe Back

Fig. 47 Louis XV Armchair Upholstered in Blue Velvet

Fig. 48

Fig. 49

Figs. 48, 49, 50, 51
Louis XV Occasional Chairs

Fig. 50

64

Fig. 51

Fig. 52

Fig. 53

Figs. 52, 53, 54, 55
Louis XVI Occasional Chairs

Fig. 54

Fig. 55

Fig. 56

Fig. 58

Fig. 57

Figs. 56, 57, 58
Louis XVI Armchairs

Figs. 59, 60, 61, 62
Directoire (top) and Empire
Occasional Chairs

66

Fig. 59

Fig. 60

Fig. 61

Fig. 62

67

Fig. 63

Fig. 64

Fig. 65

Figs. 63, 64, 65
Louis XV Chairs of
Beechwood with Rush Seats

Figs. 66, 67, 68
Empire (top) and
Louis XVI Side Chairs

Fig. 66

Fig. 67

Fig. 68

69

Fig. 69

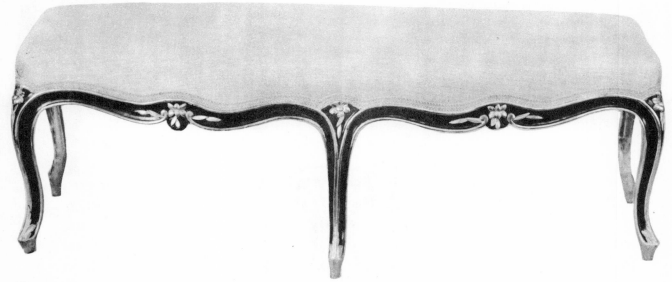

Fig. 70

Fig. 71

Figs. 69, 70, 71
Louis XV Taboret and Bench.
Louis XVI Taboret (bottom)

CHAPTER VIII

Chests and Commodes

HEN a family of Old France acquired more possessions than could be worn at one time, six oak planks were pegged together to make a chest. The advantage of this crude form of storage was that when a pillaging army approached a man could pick up his chest and run. Later the chest acquired another use. In it was accumulated the trousseau of the daughter of the family and the chest with its contents was transported after marriage to the bride's new home. As peace became more assured and prosperity increased, these chests grew larger, heavier, and were ornamented with beautiful carving.

In the northern, western and southern parts of France the motifs of the carvings were deep-cut and geometrical, in other localities they repeated the flowers, leaves and fruits of the native province. Handsome and ingenious iron or steel hinges, and locks with keys were added, but these useful and ornamental additions were always subservient to the design of the carving. Thus structure, carving and closings united to create a handsome well-proportioned, though massive, whole.

Eventually the chest acquired low legs, but it was not until the famous cabinet-maker favored by Louis XIV—Boulle—began to work that the chest was divided into convenient drawers. However, in Brittany, Alsace and in the lands along the Pyrenees, the chest in its original form maintained its popularity through many decades.

After the chest acquired legs and drawers it was christened "commode", though it continued to be referred to as a "chest of two drawers" or "chest of three drawers" as the case might be. In America, this piece of furniture is erroneously called "bureau". The term "bureau" in the parlance of Old France was given to a table with one drawer extending across the length of one side.

After Boulle had perfected and made the commode popular and when families were securely settled in their homes, the commode was developed into one of the most beautiful pieces of furniture to which the provincial cabinet-maker lent his genius.

The commode of the Régence period is massive and handsome. It stands on hoof-feet and frequently has bombé sides or a serpentine front. When it has two drawers there is often a decorative valance between the front legs with an important central ornament such as a shell or mask carved in it. Often this is pierced and cleverly heightens its grace. The metal pulls on the drawers and the keyholes are important. The light-cut carving moves around them, and thus creates a fine sense of unity. Occasionally these commodes have a top of dark grey or rose marble. They are made of both oak and walnut in their darkest hues.

During the time of Louis XV and thereafter, the commode was frequently made of fruitwood. The serpentine front became more popular, carving was more profuse, the drawer-pulls and locks were smaller and the legs were cabriole. The top was made of either marble or wood.

The commode was made in many sizes. The larger pieces usually measured about four feet long, and stood about three feet high. A "petite commode" was introduced which often measured as little as twelve inches wide. It had two or three shallow drawers and stood on high, slender, curved legs. Sometimes the feet were ornamented with metal tips or carvings called "sabots".

Another piece which came in vogue at this time was the "semanier", or "chiffonier" and was intended to be placed in the bedroom. This was a tall (about five feet) narrow chest of seven drawers. The majority of these pieces were simply constructed with no carving on either drawer-fronts or sides, and stood on low curved legs.

Toward the end of the 18th Century the commode, along with other furniture, followed the trend to the classic line. The frame was straight, sometimes the top was supported by fluted stiles. The legs were either round, fluted and straight or were vase-shaped. The only carving appeared on the drawers and consisted of a simple groove which served to make a recessed panel that harmonized with the straight lines of the frame. The drawer-pulls were of bronze and were simple half-rectangles. The escutcheons were of the same metal and appeared in the form of small bowknots, flower-baskets and other typical motifs. The tops were of wood or of grey marble.

The *petite commode* continued to be in favor and gained in delicacy and charm. It stood on high fluted legs.

In addition to fruitwood the commodes were now made of mahogany. When a marble top was added it was often white. On the *semaniers* and the *petite commodes* a gallery of pierced metal was applied. The drawer-pulls were rectangular and the escutcheons small and simple in design. Sometimes metal bands, intricately chased, encircled the top and bottom of the stiles that followed the sides and continued into the legs. Later, dainty lengths of flowers molded of metal were inserted in the flutes of the stiles near the top. These classic lines and decorations were continued through the brief Directoire period when mahogany for both commode and semanier became increasingly popular.

The commode of the Empire period was massive, its proportions heavy, and it was made of highly polished mahogany. Fruitwood was frequently used, never oak and seldom walnut. The legs were square, sometimes formed as a claw or a bun. Half-round columns were applied on the front between top and legs. There was no carving on these mahogany pieces, the only decoration being the metal mounts for drawer-pulls and keyholes with occasionally a group of laurel-leaves applied along the apron. A valanced front lightly carved with a characteristic Empire detail is seen on the commodes made of fruitwood and also on those which were painted.

Toward the close of the 18th Century and through the Empire period there was an increasing application of paint. The colors were chiefly bone-white, oyster-grey and a light green. The architecture of the piece was emphasized with narrow lines of a contrasting color such as blue, green and later, yellow.

The *semanier* now increased in width. Its construction and metal mountings followed the style of the commode previously described. White marble tops were applied frequently. The application of mirrors and glass in the doors of chiffoniers, as well as cupboards, became frequent.

The Provincials did not accept readily the style of the Empire. They continued to prefer the styles of their kings, consequently the mahogany pieces introduced at this time cannot rightly be called French Provincial though they were made for the country houses of Napoleon's "nouveau riche".

Fig. 72 Empire Bronze Keyhole

Fig. 73 Regence Bombé Commode of Walnut

Fig. 74 Louis XV Two-drawer Commode of Walnut

Fig. 75 Louis XV Three-drawer Commode of Fruitwood with Heavy Brass Escutcheons

Fig. 77 Directoire Two-drawer Commode of Walnut

Fig. 76 Louis XVI Mahogany Commode with Marble Top

Fig. 78 Empire Mahogany Commode with Standing Mirror

75

Fig. 79

Fig. 80

Fig. 82

Fig. 81

Figs 79, 80, 81, 82
Louis XV and Louis XVI
Small Commodes

CHAPTER IX

Couches and Benches

LONG, narrow oak plank from which a sprawling peg-leg protruded at every corner was the first bench used in the provinces. From this crude construction the genius of the French craftsmen developed the beautiful couches whose frames flow like waves.

In the beginning, a long oak bench was set beside the trestle table and used for eating. As the family became more numerous, it was pieced out with crude stools of similar construction. Eventually the bench acquired a back. The top rail was carved with geometric motifs and sometimes spindles were inserted between seat and top rail.

The next style to make its appearance was a long settee with a rush seat. It had a ladder-back and open arms. It was usually made of beech or ash. Eventually a flat pad of homespun or cotton was tied on it as a bid for comfort.

Heavier upholstery came in with the period of Louis XIV. Both seat and back are padded, the legs end in scrolls and the S-shaped stretcher appears between them. They are massive and possess great dignity.

The settees of the Régence period are very beautiful and possess an air of casual elegance. The frames are square but tastefully carved with shell and foliage. The backs are caned and a pad is usually placed on the caned seat.

The frames of the couches of the Louis XV period present a charming, graceful, serpentine line. The wooden frame extends above the upholstery and they have a valance which repeats the curves of the upper section. These frames are carved with cadences of flowers and vines. The cabriole leg is always present and sometimes a wing is placed at either end and the couch is then called "à oreille", that is, a "couch with ears."

The frames of the couches made in the Louis XVI style are slender and straight. The carving consists of reeding, rope or ribboned-bands, and the rosette. The upholstery is trim and flat. The legs are straight and fluted and later become vase-shaped. Oak, walnut and fruitwood were the favored woods until this time, but a fashion for painted woods developed.

The chaise longue was popular during the Régence. It had several variations. It might be one-piece. Then the head portion is somewhat higher than the foot, with a long section between. Like Régence chairs the seat, back and foot were caned.

The chaise longue of the Louis XV period follows much the same lines as the chairs. Occasionally the chair and the taboret portion is separate; or it may be made in three sections, a large high back chair, a taboret, and a smaller chair with a lower back. These fit together to form one piece of furniture or may be used separately.

The same structure applies to the chaise of Louis XVI style. It follows the classic straight lines of the period, the frames being slender and straight.

Another form of seat is the "marquise". It is made along the same lines as a chair but actually one-and-a-half seats wide.

The progression of the couch shows that from the time of Louis XV, the tendency was to reduce the amount of the wooden frame which showed. The Empire style reversed this order. The upholstery was decreased in importance, and the frame became conspicuous. Fruitwood and mahogany were employed in the construction. Lacquer in tones of white and grey was frequently used. The back of the couch is ofttimes scrolled. The legs are straight and turned, only slightly curved. The moldings are heavy. The foot is a bun, or claw. The supports may be the winged griffin, caryatid or swan. Metal mounts in period motifs were applied. A couch typical of the Empire has no back but a high scroll end with a lower scroll footboard. The chaise longue became a chair with elongated seat and no foot-board. The emphasis was not on comfort nor grace, but upon formality and drama.

Fig. 83 Carved Ornament

Fig. 84 Régence Settee of Oak with Cane Seat and Back. Upholstered with Loose Pad

Fig. 85 Régence Couch with Carved Oak Frame

Fig. 86 Louis XV Settee with Frame of Carved Walnut Upholstered in Gros Point

Fig. 87 Louis XV Couch with Enclosed Arm

Fig. 88 Louis XVI Couch with Walnut Frame

80

Fig. 89 Directoire Settee with Loose Cushion

Fig. 90

Fig. 91

Fig. 92

Figs. 90, 91, 92
Régence (top) Louis XV (center)
Louis XVI (bottom) Chaise Longues

81

Fig. 93

Fig. 94

Figs. 93, 94, 95
Empire Couches

Fig. 95

CHAPTER X

Desks and Secretaries

DURING the 17th and 18th Centuries, there developed in France a vogue for writing letters, memoirs, and word-portraits which reached the proportions of an epidemic. This fashion for letter-writing is delightfully represented by those of Madame de Sevigné to her beloved daughter, the Comtesse de Grignan, who upon her marriage left Paris to reside at the manor of her husband in Provénce. These letters are not merely charming and amusing; they not only give a vivid picture of the times; they are literature. One cannot really know the life of France until one knows the letters of Madame de Sevigné.

Memoirs, journals, and diaries, were an important part of the daily schedule of both men and women. And a favorite diversion was the writing of "portraits" in which the character, appearance, and talents (or lack of them) of one's friends and acquaintances were set down. A typical example of these "word-portraits" may be found today in the novel, *The Princess of Cleves* by Madame de La Fayette. It was then the custom to read these "portraits" at gatherings of friends. They—as well as amusing and clever letters—were sent by post, with accompanying comments and gossip, to other friends who were sojourning at their country houses, or at court, as the case might be. The "chain-letter" was truly an invention of Old France, and must have been especially delightful in times when newspapers were non-existent and travel slow and difficult.

This interest in writing gave a new impetus to the craftsmen and the desk became an important feature of every home. The French craftsman developed it in a myriad of practical and decorative forms.

The first desk used by the French was a square or rectangular table with straight columnar legs between which stretchers were inserted to strengthen them. A long, shallow drawer was placed along one side. In the business office and counting-house the top of this table-desk was covered with a piece of woolen fabric called "buria". Eventually this piece of furniture adopted the name "bureau", which was derived from the name of the fabric.

When writing became a popular diversion the functional desk of the business man developed into a long, rectangular table, with drawers in the valance, the top sometimes covered with insets of leather. The fashion for this flat-top desk received a new impetus during the reign of Louis XIV, when the cabinet-maker, Boulle, conceived the idea of eliminating the stretcher between the legs and of adding a short valance along the length of one side and drawers at either end. This afforded a convenient space for the knees and provided storage room.

When the rococo style of Louis XV took possession of France, the desk was produced in many new forms, such as the type called, "bonheur de jour". This consisted of a small rectangular table with cabriole legs and a serpentine valance. The top folded outward to provide more writing space. Across the back was placed a section with glazed or grilled doors in which books might be kept. There was also a long, shallow, screen-like piece of furniture, on which the top portion opened outward to provide space for writing. Beneath this folding leaf, small cupboards were arranged to hold stationery and writing supplies. These charming little desks usually measure about three to four feet long, but are not more than 12 inches deep. They stand on legs and can easily be moved about.

During the period of Louis XV the slant-front desk, with one or two long drawers beneath the writing section, became popular. These are usually made of walnut or fruitwood. They have the cabriole leg and the decorative escutcheons and drawer-pulls typical of the period. A tall section to hold books was sometimes placed above the writing section of this slant-front desk. In construction and ornament, these tall pieces were similar to the *armoires* and buffets.

The restrained carving, smaller pulls and escutcheons and the straight, fluted leg which characterizes the style Louis XVI was applied to desks as to other pieces of furniture and with the arrival of the Directoire and Empire eras, mahogany became a favorite wood. The slant-front became a cylinder and the interior, covered by a rounded lid, was fitted with many small drawers.

Another form was introduced at this time. It was a tall, flat rectangle with a long drawer extending across the top, in the center was a leaf which could be opened outward to provide writing space. The inner compartment was fitted with many small drawers. The lower section had two or three long drawers reaching across the width of the piece or this lower section was enclosed in two cupboard-like doors. It stood on low fluted legs. Fluted stiles rose on either side of the piece and continued to the short legs. During the Directoire period, these legs were often vase-shaped. Sometimes bands of metal encircled the stiles at top and bottom. A marble plateau with a gallery of pierced brass was frequently added.

On the more elegant pieces, marquetry in designs of bow knots and bouquets ornamented the front. The woods used were fruitwood, walnut, mahogany and as the 18th Century neared its close, lacquer became popular.

The desk and secretaries of the Empire period followed the same forms; that is, they were long, rectangular tables with drawers on either side, or they were tall secretaries with a falling-leaf provided for writing. Light colored fruitwood and mahogany were used in their construction. The foot was a bun, a claw or a short angular leg finished the piece. The stiles were often half-round columns. Both desks and secretaries were ornamented with typical Napoleonic motifs in the form of carvings or metal appliqués and had the massive, cumbersome proportions characteristic of this period.

Fig. 96 Louis XV Bronze Keyhole

Fig. 97 Louis XIV Boulle Desk Inlaid with Tortoise Shell and Metal

Fig. 98 Louis XV Walnut Dropfront Desk with Drawers

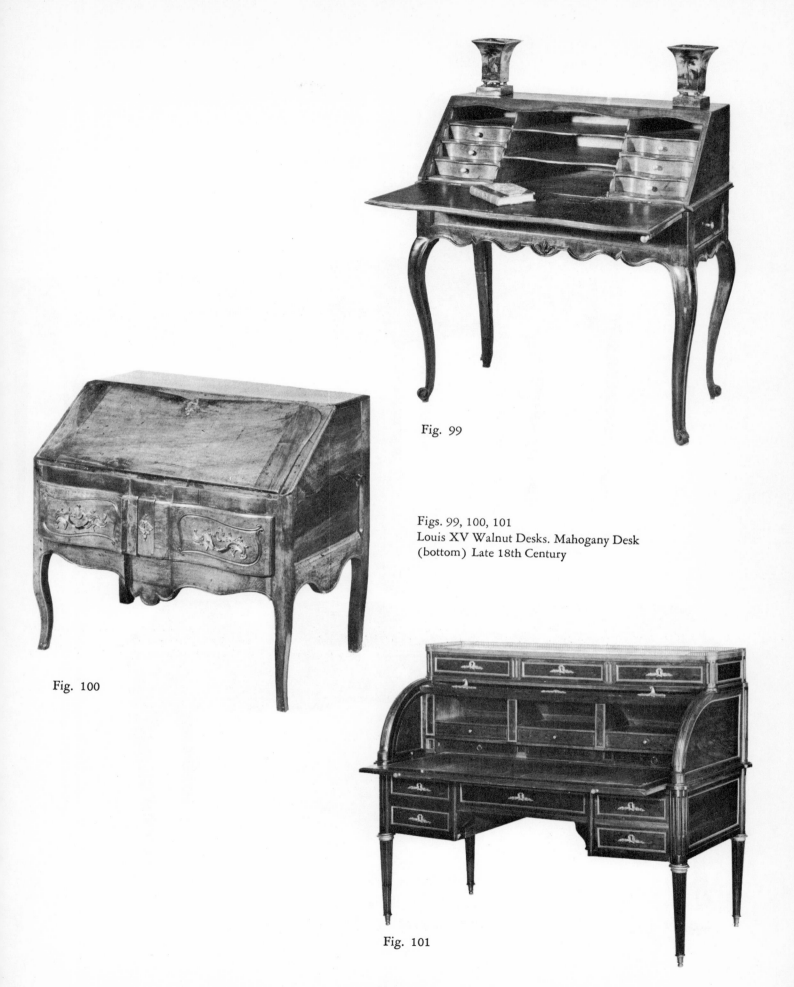

Fig. 99

Figs. 99, 100, 101
Louis XV Walnut Desks. Mahogany Desk
(bottom) Late 18th Century

Fig. 100

Fig. 101

Fig. 102

Fig. 103

Figs. 102, 103
Louis XV and Louis XVI (top) Writing Tables

Fig. 104 Louis XV Lacquer Secretary with Fall-front

Fig. 105 Secretary made of Fruitwood with Drawers.
Late 18th Century

Fig. 106 Louis XVI Mahogany Secretary with Bookcases

Fig. 107 Empire Mahogany Secretary Ornamented with Bronze Mounts

CHAPTER XI

Tables

HE first tables used by the Provincials consisted of a trestle over which a long narrow board was laid. Eventually the legs became attached to the table and were straight or turned into knobs. During the time of Louis XIII the legs were carved into spirals and balusters, while in the following reign, they acquired an S-shaped stretcher.

However, furniture was so precious that it seemed extravagant for a table to be used for eating only. Consequently, a trough was sometimes built beneath the top and was used for both the making and storing of bread. The sides of the trough were carved with leaves, flowers and shells, sometimes the top board, which was removable, was scalloped. The piece then assumed both a decorative and utilitarian purpose.

During the time of the Régence, the table developed a multitude of variations. It was made in many sizes, from large to diminutive, and became lighter and more graceful in construction. The stretcher between the legs was abandoned because it gave an appearance of weight. The legs curved, sometimes ended in a dainty hoof, and the apron was carved with motifs of shell and foliage. Marble tops were applied.

In Normandy, especial attention was given to the sides of the table. They were made with valances that were beautifully carved, frequently drawers were inserted and handsome brass pulls added. The next invention was pull-out leaves. These rested beneath the top, when opened, they permitted the table to be extended several feet. However, the drop-leaf table on swinging legs, so popular among English and American cabinet-makers, was seldom made in France.

With the advance of the 18th Century the table followed the lead of all other furniture, and adopted the rococo curve and cabriole leg termed "Style Louis XV". Fruitwood now had precedence over oak and walnut which were the woods previously favored for tables. Refinements in structure were developed and also many new types were originated.

The dining tables of this period are usually rectangular. They have a scalloped apron and cabriole leg which is carved at the top joinings. The drawers have scalloped panels and large decorative brass pulls.

The occasional tables are myriad. They stand on high curved legs. A popular type was one with sides enclosed a third of the way down from the top. The front portion was open, affording a convenient resting place for books or embroidery. These tables frequently had marble tops which rested within the sides that rose up a couple of inches to end in a scalloped or shaped molding.

One of the most charming of the many kinds of small tables of the Louis XV period was called "Refraichissoir". A shelf was inserted between the cabriole legs about one-third of the height from the floor. The top was marble with two wells cut into it in which were inserted metal-liners for wine coolers.

Another type of small table had a screen placed at the back. This screen consisted of a molding which was fitted with a piece of fabric or needlepoint, could be raised or lowered, as desired. Shallow drawers were placed along the front. When this table was put before the hearth it served as a receptacle for sewing and also as a fire-screen. Small "sabot" feet were often carved as a finish for the legs.

From the time of Louis XIV the French cherished a great fondness for the console table and later for the large center table. In the beginning these tables had deep, heavily carved valances, but their construction became lighter, the carving more restrained, as the years passed. Console tables were made of oak, walnut, and less frequently of fruitwood. The center tables were similarly made and in the later years had a top covered with tooled leather.

With the introduction of the style Louis XVI the legs of the tables became straight and fluted. Sometimes the legs were tapering columns with the top carved in classic designs. In wood, shape, size, and structure, these tables repeated the types of the earlier reign but now a new wood became popular—mahogany. Vase-shaped legs, metal bands and beadings became general during the Directoire period but, for the most part, no important change was made.

Two new shapes appeared at the end of the 18th Century. One was the demilune console, a half-round table, with one or two drawers in the apron, and, very often, a white marble top. The more elegant pieces were ornamented with a gallery of pierced brass. Drawer pulls and key holes were delicate on both the Louis XVI and Directoire pieces. The second innovation was the introduction of a mahogany dining table, either oval or round, which could be opened for the insertion of one or two leaves.

Tables took on new life with the arrival of the Empire. Fruitwood of a sunny taffy color became popular. Many circular tables were made in both large and small sizes. The legs were slender and curved inward from the apron and then outward, sometimes ending in claw feet. Tables were also made with a deep, plain apron and mounted on legs that were thick, round columns. Metal rings and bands sometimes encircled them. The tops were occasionally of deep green or white marble.

Fig. 108 Rustic Bread-trough and Table. Early 18th Century

93

Fig. 109

Fig. 110

Figs. 109, 110, 111
17th Century (top) Louis XV and Louis XVI Dining Tables

94

Fig. 111

Fig. 112

Fig. 113

Figs. 112, 113, 114
Louis XV and Empire Console Tables

95   Fig. 114

Fig. 115

Fig. 116

Figs. 115, 116
Louis XV and Louis XVI Game Tables

Fig. 117 Louis XV Small Oak Table

Fig. 118

Fig. 119

Fig. 120

Fig. 121

Figs. 118, 119, 120, 121
Louis XV and Louis XVI Chairside Tables

Fig. 122

Figs. 122, 123, 124
Louis XIV (top) Louis XV
and Louis XVI Console Tables

Fig. 123

Fig. 124

CHAPTER XII

Conversation Pieces

FRENCH Provincial craftsmen made many charming products which were once useful but which today have no functional purpose. Yet these small pieces possess so much wit, charm and grace, that they continue as ornaments and lend character and authenticity to the contemporary room.

On the wall of every French home hung a "panetiere"—a cage for bread—it won a nostalgic description in the writings of the French novelist, Alphonse Daudet, who wrote: "That open-work cage, that precious, saucy little cage; 'tis all my country".

This "saucy little cage" in which the housewife kept her long loaves of bread was a rectangle of oak or walnut. Its sides were spindles. At top and bottom was an apron and bonnet prettily carved. It sat on the top of a buffet or hung on the wall—supreme in its importance. Though the *panetiere* has outlived its usefulness it is so typical of France that it continues to add charm to many an interior today.

Similar in form to the English knife-box was the salt-box. Salt was taxed in France and the possession of a well-filled salt-box was an indication of wealth. Therefore the salt-box was a prized possession of every living-room-kitchen and delightfully decorative. Useless, today, it is none the less charming.

Once there stood in every home of Provincial France a wall-fountain. This was a receptacle to hold water, for it must be remembered that even palaces did not have running water in the 18th Century. This fountain consisted of a cylinder made of pottery, pewter or copper, with a faucet. Below this was a basin of the same material. It stood on a bracket of wood which was attached to the wall, or it rested on a stand with a back. The stand might be only a carved panel, or the lower section might have drawers, or be a cupboard with a drawer.

The wood-carver, metal worker, and potter expended so much invention and skill in giving these pieces charm, that they are quite irresistible. The wall-fountain is so characteristic and so decorative, that like the bread-box or *panetiere,* it is still a favorite addition to all Provincial interiors. Nowadays it is often placed in hallways or in small corners and the basin is filled with flowers or greenery.

The French homemaker adored open shelves. She used them to display her favorite bits of copper, pewter and pottery, as little shrines for the statues of her Madonna or favorite Saint, and a thousand and one other uses. The craftsmen made them for her pleasure in every size and type imaginable.

There were single, narrow shelves, as long as six feet, which were placed above cabinets and tables. Hooks were put into the lower board and from them spoons and jugs were suspended. Gay plates or bright porringers rested above. Sometimes these long shelves were quite plain and then again they would be beautifully and gracefully shaped, ornamented with flower-carvings or with spindles, or even both. Of course there were shorter shelves too, and tiers of shelves. Shelves to hang on the wall in corners, over cupboards, and every place a woman can hang a shelf—and her imagination in this direction knows no horizon.

These shelves were made of oak and walnut. Toward the end of the 18th Century, and especially during the early years of the 19th Century, hanging-shelves were made of fruitwood with the bottom part enclosed by small doors which were often prettily ornamented with delicate inlays of flowers or stars. They were painted too, in beautiful shades of lacquer-red, emerald-green, and black . . . the better to display cherished bric-a-brac.

When three or more shelves were arranged in tiers with perpendicular supports the piece was called "étagère" and was constructed somewhat like the Victorian what-not. The tall single shelf on high legs was termed "guéridon" and served to hold vases, flowers, and statues. Corner shelves of walnut and fruitwood, both open and closed, were included among the products of the Provincial craftsman, these were frequently decorated with inlay or lacquer toward the middle of the 18th Century.

A charming small piece was the table called "poudreuse". It was usually about three feet long and a foot or so wide. The center panel of the top lifted to expose a mirror. Beneath this panel a well was concealed. The two side panels opened outward and revealed additional wells in which cosmetics were kept. Shallow drawers were sometimes placed beneath these wells. The *poudreuse* was popular during the Louis XV and Louis XVI eras and was usually made of walnut or fruitwood, though in the later years of the century it came to be lacquered.

Unusual small pieces of furniture are continually turning up and are invariably welcomed with delight. They always seem to possess a function, though frequently their usefulness is far removed from the purpose which sponsored their production.

Fig. 125 Louis XV Pewter Wall-fountain with Dolphin Spout and Embossed Design

Fig. 126 Louis XV Panetière of Walnut

Fig. 127 Louis XV Brass Wall-fountain on
an Oak Panel with Cupboard

Fig. 128 Louis XV Standing Shelves
with Glazed Door

Fig. 129 Louis XVI Mahogany Table
with Shelves for Ornaments

Fig. 130 Régence Carved Oak Wall Bracket

Fig. 131 Rustique Cradle of Oak. 18th Century

104

CHAPTER XIII

French Provincial in Canada
1613~1870

BEYOND the boundaries of France there was another province which continued the great tradition of her craftsmen—Canada. The fur trade, and the Jesuit's zeal to convert the Indians, was the reason for the settlement of this far land. The first group of adventurers and priests arrived during the early years of the 17th Century, but it was not until the Iroquois went on the war path and threatened to extinguish the colony that the Mother Country took much interest in the courageous project. Then in 1660 a regiment of troops was sent to Canada to maintain order and a truly great priest, Monseigneur de Laval, was called to make the Church self-sustaining. He began by establishing a school of arts and crafts at Cap Tourmente which continued to flourish well into the 19th Century. There a unique and beautiful folk art developed, which fused rustic simplicity and strength with the classic elegance and grace of the cultured land which was the source of its tradition.

The purpose of the teachers and students was primarily to beautify the churches but the skills which were acquired gradually penetrated into the new homes. Thus the building and decoration of the churches of Canada performed the same service as did that of the palaces of France. They trained the hands, educated the eyes of the people, inspired their imagination to accomplishment and stimulated their desire for possession.

One of the most charming crafts to develop was needlework. The Ursuline nuns taught the Indian women to embroider. Soon the same motifs which adorned the palaces of Louis XIV appeared on the cradle-boards of papooses. The women from France and their daughters carried over their knowledge of church embroideries to their bedspreads, draperies and rugs.

The daughters of both Native and Settler were industrious students of a curriculum which included "good French manners, housekeeping, needlework, drawing, painting, music, some notions of architecture and other fine arts".

The men of the colony, under the direction of the priests, became adept at masonry, carpentry, cabinet-making, plaster-work, metal-work, lock-making and wood-sculpture. Every student of advanced theology and the arts was required to learn a craft. However, many of the men, even before coming to Canada to establish their fortunes and families, were accomplished craftsmen trained under the rigorous and righteous system of the old French guilds. Today you may find the same names in the French records of the medieval guilds duplicated in the telephone books of Montreal and Quebec. These eleventh and twelfth generation French-Canadians are proud of their guild-ancestry and rightly so.

Cut off from their homeland by a wide and treacherous sea, these valiant men and women from France gradually divided themselves into two groups—the "habitants", who farmed the land, and the townspeople, who earned a livelihood from the practice of the trades and the professions. Little or no interest in their welfare was shown by France. Occasionally the gift of a statue or chalice or candelabra would be made to a church, but the buildings and furnishings of the homes were the work of the settlers' own hands and wits. They lived a happy-go-lucky life, completely free of mercenary ambition—working hard by day, playing hard by night, and on Sundays praying devoutly. Bounded on the one hand by the far horizons of an ocean and on the other by a virgin forest of unknown extent, they lived on a planet all their own. To them beauty and art were not luxuries . . . they were necessities. For culture is never superimposed; it must exist within. These French-Canadians possessed it and further developed it to an admirable degree.

The furniture first made in Canada followed the symmetrical style of the period of Louis XIV, for that was the vogue when the settlers left Europe. They continued it long after it was obsolete in France, for transportation and communication were slow and uncertain. But fashion has wings and as the 18th Century came into swing, a lighter rococo style became popular, especially in the towns. This was followed, toward the close of the century, by the classic style which had attained great popularity in France during the period of Louis XVI. The Empire style which followed in France attained little recognition among Canadian craftsmen.

106

These styles were adapted to the materials and needs of the new country. By and large, the same articles used in France were made for the homes of Canada—chests, armoires, buffets, commodes, beds, tables, chairs and stools. Their shapes were square and rectangular, ornamented with deep-cut moldings. The motifs employed by the habitant were geometrical even into the 18th Century when the townspeople had adopted the Louis XV curve and the shell. As the century progressed, the tops of cupboards, chairs and beds became rounded. The panels of doors were carved with baskets of fruit and with flowers, but so simply rendered as to be almost stylized. They were never carved with the realistic and elaborate detail favored in France. The wood used was pine. This was given a lustrous wax finish. The chairs and tables were frequently painted red. The oak and fruitwoods so popular overseas seemed not to attract the Canadian craftsmen nor were they sufficiently available for his use. When ships from the West Indies began to sail into port in the later years of the 18th Century and during the 19th Century, mahogany came into occasional use.

The production of decorative accessories was prolific. Women wove colorful draperies, bedspreads and upholstery of wool, linen and finally of cotton. Their dyes were made from flowers and herbs culled in their doorstep gardens. The motifs were geometric and stylized interpretations of flowers, fruits and birds. During the 19th Century they began to make the hooked-rug which now attracts so many tourists to Canada. In the beginning the designs of these rugs were delightfully naive and their colors were well-chosen. After the conquest by the British (1763) the making of numerous boxes and dishes of birch-bark beautifully embroidered with dyed porcupine-quills was begun. Many minor crafts developed about this time—leather-work, book-binding, artificial flowers, wax-fruit and hair-pictures. But the gem of all the crafts created by the women of Canada was their embroideries. They bear the stamp of genius.

Among the Ursuline nuns who taught in the schools were several who were descendants of French families who had long been active in the textile trade. To Montreal came Madame Marie de l'Incarnation who was the daughter of a silk merchant of Tours, a descendant of the famous family of Babons le Bourdaisiere who had assisted in establishing tapestry-making in France under Frances I and whose shop later became a part of the Gobelins. There were the gifted Mere Saint Joseph and Madame de la Petrie from Alençon, the city of fine laces. In Quebec, the talented Jeanne Le Ber trained in the cloister from 1647-1677, wrought miracles with threads. She inspired the French-Canadian girls to glorious accomplishment.

As embroidery was the chosen craft for women, so silversmithy was the craft in which men excelled and it is possible to identify by name many of the Canadian craftsmen. They are worthy of being accorded equal honors with leaders of the craft in England, America and France.

The first silversmith known to have worked in Canada was Michael Levasseur who established his shop in Quebec in 1698. In the first years of the 18th Century there were many smiths in both Montreal and Quebec, most of whom had been trained in France—Paul Lambert of Arras, France; Roland Paradis of Paris and Ignace Delezenne of Lille, who originated the idea of making Indian trade silver after 1763 and thereby became a very rich man. Michael Cotton and François Landron were born in Quebec, as was the greatest genius of them all—François Ranvoyse. Fine work was also done by Huguet, Marion, Cruickshank and Morand. During the second half of the century the silver craft was dominated by Laurent Amiot, born in Quebec. Though he died in 1839, his style was continued by his apprentices and the shop he founded was not closed until 1905.

Silver was greatly in demand for church and for home use, even though the colonial economic policy of France did not encourage it. After 1763 when the wars with Indians and British ended and the country became more prosperous, silvercraft came into its full flowering.

In the beginning the smithys followed the true and pure tradition of Provincial Louis XIV. Later a classic revival was inaugurated by Amiot. The pieces made for homes consisted of cups, porringers, ewers, basins, platters, bowls and flatware. They are masterpieces of line and proportion. Their ornament is conceived with splendid originality and brilliantly executed.

Prosperity killed this fine craft. When Delezenne began to make silver ornaments for the fur traders to use in bartering pelts with the Indians, the demand for silver grew by leaps and bounds. Quality gave place to quantity. Some fine home and church silver continued to appear but the Grand Epoch of Canadian Silversmithy ended.

Fig. 132 Gold Applique. Late 18th Century

Fig. 133 Dark Brown Painted Table with Drawer

Fig. 134 Prie-Dieu of Pine. Circa 1695

Fig. 135 Monk's Bench from the Province of Quebec

109

Fig. 136 Buffet of Pine with Deep Geometric
Carvings. 18th Century

Fig. 137 Buffet of Pine with Two Closed
Doors. Late 18th Century

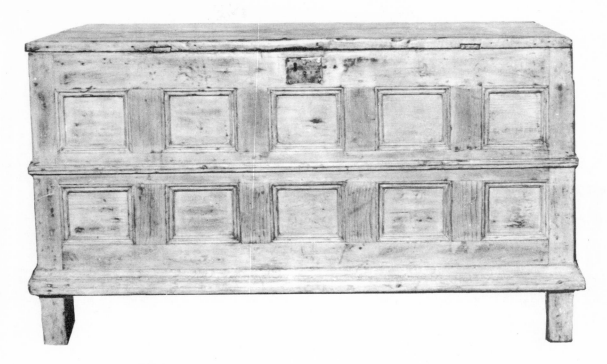

Fig. 138 Carved Pine Chest

Fig. 139 Commode of Pine. 18th Century
(Contemporary Pulls)

Fig. 140 Commode of Pine with Marquetry.
Louis XV Style

111

Fig. 141 Corner Cupboard in Two Parts
with Glazed Doors. Circa 1800

Fig. 142 Armoire with Two Doors

112

Fig. 143 Double-tiered Unpainted
Pine Cupboard. 18th Century

Fig. 144 Vestry-cupboard of Pine. 18th Century

113

Fig. 145 Turned Spool Armchair with
Rush Seat. 17th Century

Fig. 146

Figs. 146, 147
Painted Wood Chairs. 18th Century

Fig. 147

Figs. 148, 149, 150 Church Ornaments

Fig. 148 Carved Wood Candlestick

Fig. 149 Carved Wood Flower Basket

Fig. 150 Embroidered Altar Frontal

Fig. 151 Silver Porringer, Roland Paradis

Fig. 152 Silver Porringer. Roland Paradis

Fig. 154 Tureen. Robert Cruickshank

Fig. 153 Silver Porringer. Probably by Joseph Mailloux

Fig. 155 Tureen. Laurent Amyot

116

Fig. 156 Silver Spoons. Probably by Michael Cotton

Fig. 157 Silver Ewer. Probably by Laurent Amyot

Fig. 158 Silver Ladle. Jonas Schindler

Fig. 159 Silver Tray with Engraved Border

Fig. 160 Tin Candlesticks Painted Pink
and Green. Early 19th Century

Fig. 161 Carved Wood Chandelier

Fig. 162 Pine Cradle

Fig. 163 Carved and Painted Cradle Board

118

DECORATIVE ARTS

1700 ～ 1820

Ranson del.

Berthaut sc.

Fig. 164 Decorative Arts of the Late 17th and Early 18th Centuries

Fig. 165 Decorative Arts of the Middle 18th Century

Fig. 166 Decorative Arts of the Last Quarter of the 18th Century

Fig. 167 Decorative Arts of the Late 18th and Early 19th Centuries

Fig. 168 Design for Empire Ceiling

Fig. 169 Empire Morning Room

CHAPTER XIV

Mantels and Fireplace Fixtures

HE fireplace of the French home was the heart of the house. It performed two important functions . . . it supplied heat and in it food was cooked. In early times, it also supplied light, for it pieced out, in welcome measure, the fickle glow of candle and lamp. Its size was determined by the local weather and the cooking requirements of the family. Later, as prosperity increased and rooms were added to the original living-room-kitchen, the fireplace diminished in size and served only as a source of heat. The appearance of mantel and fixtures changed with function.

The fireplace, when Henry IV wished for a fowl in the pot every Sunday, was a masonry chimney with a mouth. Across the mouth a beam of wood was inserted as a prop for the stones and also as an attachment for hooks from which hung cooking wares and implements. In the colder climes, crude benches and stools stood right in the fireplace so that all the precious heat could be enjoyed.

Usually the fireplace occupied one entire wall of the home. In milder climates, a corner fireplace was built. This presented a rounded chimney breast which extended from wall to wall and then rose from the mouth to the ceiling in a cone shape.

When the purpose of the hearth came to be heat only, mantels became decorative. The mantels during the times of Henry IV and Louis XIII were square, massive, and in prosperous homes, heavily carved. The mantel of the Louis XIV period consisted of two simple, heavy scrolls which extended upward and outward from the wall and across which a deep shelf was placed. These mantels were made of oak, stone, or, in the more elegant manors, they came to be made of marbles of dark color.

With the arrival of the style Louis XV the woodcarver came into his own. From walnut, and occasionally from fruitwoods, he fashioned graceful mantels. The line of the opening was serpentine and rose to a decorative shell motif. Over the surface of the wood the favorite rococo motifs of period and locale were carved. These mantels were made both with and without an overhanging shelf. Though the mantel was decorative and an important feature of the room in which it was placed it was not as large as that favored in English homes of this time. In France the mantel was intended to remain a harmonious part of the décor rather than a dominating feature. Oftentimes it appeared to be a functional part of the panelling. When the wall was covered with wood it continued the design and conformed to the proportions of the wall-covering. Mirrors were often set above the mantel, clocks and barometers were also placed on the wall directly above the hearth.

During the Louis XVI period mantels became smaller. Their surface was fluted and the juncture of side and shelf was marked by a rosette. Marble became popular and was used both in white and grey. As the use of lacquer on furniture and on walls increased in popularity, mantelpieces were painted in the favorite colors of blue, oyster-white, gray or a soft green and thus harmonized with the decorative scheme of the room.

The Empire mantel consisted of flat slabs of dark green or black or chalk-white marble. If wood, it was mahogany or lacquer that was preferred. It repeated the design of the furniture; columns, half-rounds, and caryatids were used. At times it was ornamented with bronze appliqués in period motifs.

Fireplaces were ornamented with firebacks of iron. These plates were molded with varied designs such as escutcheons, religious and mythological symbols.

In the summer, when the fireplace was not used, the French added a charming decorative note to their rooms by placing a screen before the vacant hearth. The fire-screen of the Louis XIV period was of wrought iron and was similar in design to that used on the exterior balconies of the house. From the Régence period downward, the firescreen usually had a frame of oak or walnut. This followed the typical form and designs of the period and the frames were handsomely carved. Panels of fabric, gros point or petit point were inserted in them. Toward the end of the 18th Century and on into the 19th Century, decorative wallpaper panels were placed in the frames at which time the name was changed to fireboard.

Fig. 170 Louis XIV Marble Mantel

Fig. 171 Louis XV Walnut Mantel

Fig. 172 Louis XVI Marble Mantel

Fig. 173 Empire Fruitwood Mantel

Fig. 174 Louis XVI Andiron of
Bronze-Doré with Urn Finial

Fig. 175 Louis XV Andiron of Bronze with
Shepherd in Rococo Swirl

Fig. 176 Bronze Fire Screen. Early 19th Century

Fig. 177

Fig. 178

Fig. 179

Fig. 180 Louis XIV Iron Fire Screen

Figs. 177, 178, 179
Fire Screens with Carved Walnut Frames
Inset with Tapestry Panels.
Early 18th Century

131

Fig. 181 Designs for Mantelpieces

132

CHAPTER XV

Mirrors

fountain in every garden; a mirror in every room—this is a basic rule of French décor. The brilliance and sparkle, the fascinating play of light and shade, the effervescent gaiety and changing reflections of playing water and of mirrored glass, are harmonious with the French joie de vivre.

The first mirror known to have entered France was carried from Italy three centuries ago over the Apennines on mule-back. It still hangs in the palace of Fontainebleau in the room where Marie de Medici, wife of Henry IV, gave birth to her first son, destined to rule France as Louis XIII.

The use of mirrors in decoration was given impetus when Louis XIV built the palace of Versailles. The magnificent long gallery, facing the gardens, was lined from floor to ceiling with giant mirrors. It was in this famous "Galerie des Glaces" that the Germans in 1870 forced the French to sign the articles of capitulation following the disastrous Franco-Prussian war, and there in 1918, victorious France and her Allies signed the Treaty of Versailles.

Though the mirror was an established feature in the palaces of 17th Century France, it was not until the first part of the 18th Century that it came into general use. Then a method of pouring plate glass was discovered and the mirror launched on a

133

fertile career. Both form and frame were developed by the carvers in characteristic fashion through the five great periods of French décor.

The mirrors of the Louis XIV period are square. Often bands of mirror are inserted in the heavily and deeply carved frames. The whole is surmounted by an imposing cluster of martial trophies or a sunburst. They are richly gilded. But this fashion had little influence upon the Provincial craftsmen because plate-glass was scarce.

The Régence saw a more general use of the mirror. It became rectangular in shape. Just as the carving of wall panelling and picture frames became more restrained, so also did the frames for mirrors. Gilding was discarded and the dark tones of walnut and oak made a striking contrast with the brilliance of the glass. The surface of the wood was lightly carved with intricate strapwork or rocaille design. When motifs appear on the top and in the corners of the frame they present a shell or mask. The effect is one of elegance and dignity.

Mirrors—as did so many other types of furnishings—enjoyed a full effulgence during the reign of Louis XV. Then the inventive genius of the wood carver went its gamut. The frames were carved with trailing vines and flowers. In the more rustic types, the top of the mirror frame was carved with the favorite motifs of the home-province such as sprays of laurel leaves, hearts, musical instruments, large acanthus leaves, scrolls, etc. Garlands of realistic flowers were festooned over the top. The wood (walnut or fruitwoods) was usually left in its natural state, or lightly and softly gilded.

Mirrors of the Louis XVI period follow the general tendency to classical restraint. The shape became a tall rectangle. The frames were narrow and were carved with delicate beading, fine moldings, or a small version of the egg and dart pattern. They were also surmounted by pediments carved in the forms of doves, musical instruments, quiver and arrows. Natural wood, gilding and lacquer were the finishes of the frames.

The styles Louis XV and Louis XVI present a type of mirror that is unique to the French school. It was called a "trumeau". This mirror is usually rectangular. The frame is narrow but may be either rococo or classic in design. A painting is inserted in the upper portion. The subjects chosen were usually romantic and were often copies or adaptations of the pictures of court painters—Boucher, Watteau, Fragonard.

The mirrors of these two periods were intended to hang on the wall over commodes, consoles and mantels. In the more luxurious rooms they were frequently inset in the panels of the walls. This custom was continued until the Empire when the mirror was subjected to a decided change in style.

The mirrors of the Empire period were usually framed in wide, smooth bands of wood. A dark, highly polished mahogany was popular. To this was applied ornaments of bronze in typical Napoleonic motifs. Gilded frames were also used. These show light surface carvings in the corners and duplicate motifs are evenly spaced on the sides and top. This motif is usually a stylized strap-work medallion. A tall standing mirror came into use. The frame was a wide mahogany band, sometimes trimmed with bronze appliqués. It hung on metal pins which allowed the angle of the mirror to be adjusted. This pin was inserted in a column which extended part-way up on the sides of the mirror and which ended in feet that assured an upright position. Miniature variations of this design were placed on commodes and dressing tables.

Fig. 182 Design for Silver Mirror Frame by Pierre Germain

135

Fig. 183 Mirror with Carved Wood Frame.
Late 17th or Early 18th Century

Fig. 185 Louis XV Trumeau with Painting
in the Manner of Watteau

Fig. 184 Louis XIV Carved and Gilded Wood Frame

Fig. 187 Louis XVI Oval Mirror with Carved
Wood Frame Painted Gray

Fig. 186 Louis XVI Mirror with Carved Wooden
Frame Showing Doves and Arrows

137

Fig. 188

Fig. 190

Fig. 189

Figs. 188, 189, 190
Louis XVI Mirrors with Painted
and Gilded Carved Wood Frames

Fig. 191 Carved and Gilded Louis XVI Mirror Flanked by Sconces of Bronze-Doré

Fig. 192 Gilded Carved Wood Frame for a Circular
Mirror. Late 18th Century

139

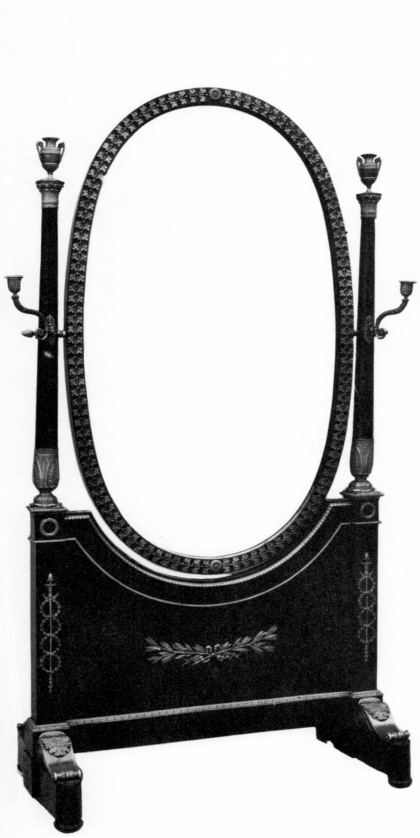

Fig. 193 Overmantel Mirror with Mahogany Frame, Carved and Gilded Decoration. Late 18th or Early 19th Century

Fig. 194 Empire Cheval Glass with Mahogany Frame and Ormulu Mounts

CHAPTER XVI

Glass

T is said that the first glass factory to be established in the world was the Imperial Factory of Frontincennes which was founded in the second century at Forêt-Eu, France. It is certain that as early as the 12th Century a prolific industry for making wine-bottles flourished in France. The stained glass windows of the Gothic cathedrals are proof of French virtuosity in this medium. Yet there exists no representative collection of glass for household use produced during the 18th Century, when the decorative arts enjoyed their greatest prosperity. A search of the records in important libraries in America, England, and France is most disappointing, and yet the very absence of product and of record presents a fascinating challenge.

A few facts are known which confirm the presence of this craft in France. For instance, there are records to prove that in 1655 Richard Lucas de Nehon founded the Manufactaire Royal des Glaces; the same year a mirror factory was established in the Faubourg St. Antoine, Paris, and to it workmen were imported from Venice; in 1688 Louis Nehon invented a method of casting glass plates which allowed the production of the material in sheets of unlimited size. His franchise states that he was "allowed to take for his partners, even nobles and ecclesiastics, without it being derogatory to their nobility". The first important recognition of the craft occurred when Louis XIV had glass set into the windows of his coach (1672) and later ordered the construction of the "Gallerie des Glaces" at Versailles.

The few pieces of glass tableware which have been preserved show that the French craftsmen followed the Venetian style—the glass was drawn thin and decorated with enamelling, splashing, and by superimposing a layer of glass on the original body. As the 18th Century advanced, glassware was engraved in designs which included stippling and graceful floral patterns and ornamented with gold. In 1815 M. Artiques established the factory of St. Anne at Baccarat where crystal and colored glasses of remarkable brilliance and clarity were produced. It was not until after this time that the beautiful millefiore paper weights, and opaline glass were developed at Baccarat and other factories, such as St. Louis and Clichy.

Until further research proves fruitful it is safe to say that glass was never put to the utilitarian purposes for which metals and ceramics were employed, but served chiefly for ornament. Glass and crystal were used as lustres to adorn lighting fixtures, for the sides of decorative lanterns, and were set into sconces. They were combined with bronze to create bowls, boxes and epergnes, and similar ornaments.

During the Louis XV and Louis XVI periods, glass was engraved and painted and in this form used as pictures. Mirror painting was popular and also a type termed "Verre églomisé". This term is a variant of an artist's name. In the second half of the 18th Century glass pictures were made by Jean Baptiste Glomy who was an artist, antiquarian and a writer on art. He painted on the under-side of glass with opaque colors, sometimes heightening his designs with gold, but always without a metallic background. Mirror pictures showing Chinese designs, both painted and engraved, were popular and a fanciful use of mirror was made by cutting engravings and applying the silhouettes of people, trees and plants to the glass to create romantic scenes which were framed as pictures.

Fig. 195 Blown, Cut and Enamelled Glass. Late 18th Century

Fig. 196
Jug of Greenish Blue and White Glass.
French or Venetian. 18th Century

Fig. 197
Tumbler, Engraved and Cut. Probably
French. 18th or 19th Century

Fig. 198
Jug, Clear Glass with Molded Ornament,
Probably French. 17th or 18th Century

Fig. 199
Bottle, Enamelled in Color.
French, 18th Century

Fig. 200
Jug, French or Venetian.
17th or 18th Century

Fig. 201
Wine Glass with French Coin of 1727
in Knob. French, 18th Century

Fig. 202 Glass Ornaments of the Early 19th Century

144

CHAPTER XVII

Clocks and Barometers

THE grandfather clock of the French Provinces was a distinguished looking patriarch. It was fashioned of oak, walnut, cherry or fruitwood along tall, stalwart lines. Even when its form assumed the rococo curve, the shape was controlled and progressed majestically upward. The case was carved with characteristic motifs of its native province and period. Taking its stand along a wall lined with armoire, buffet and *bonnetière,* it had a commanding mien.

A typical feature of French décor is the custom of affixing the clock to the wall. During the 18th Century the bracket clock came into vogue. Its case was carved into serpentine lines which were repeated in the matching bracket. Both clock and bracket were frequently painted a dark green, or copen blue and touched with gilding. Bouquets and garlands in realistic colors were painted about the face. Clocks were also encased in glass, the sides being held together with narrow strips of metal.

In the manor houses, the cases of clocks were frequently made of bronze, first fashioned in rococo scrolls and later in classic designs. Putti and other romantic figures appeared on the top and later came urns and doves. Mantels were adorned with a three-piece garniture consisting of a clock with a pair of vases or candlesticks. For these ornaments marble or semi-precious stones were combined with bronze.

145

The popular clock of the Empire period was fashioned of bronze-doré polished to a brilliant lustre. The basic form of the case was square or rectangular surmounted by a figure of a mythological personage.

During the Directoire and Empire a circular or octagonal clock resembling an oversize watch came into fashion and was hung on the wall. Its case was usually tole painted in mustard-color, black, red or dark green and ornamented with gilding and stylized motifs.

It would seem that the barometer was almost as important an adjunct to a room as was the clock, so frequently does it appear in the documentary drawings and engravings of the 18th Century. The cases followed the design and motifs of their period.

Figs. 203, 204
Louis XV and Louis XVI Barometers

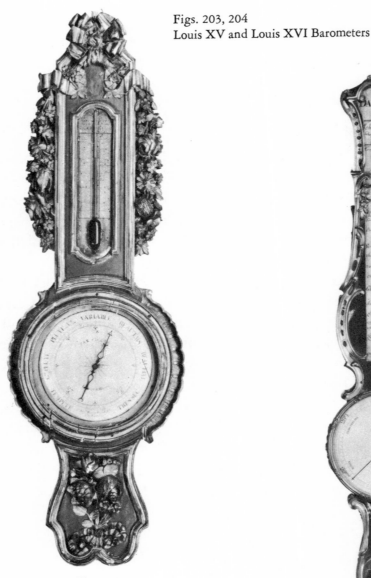

Fig. 203

Fig. 204

Fig. 205 Régence Clock with Ormulu Mounts

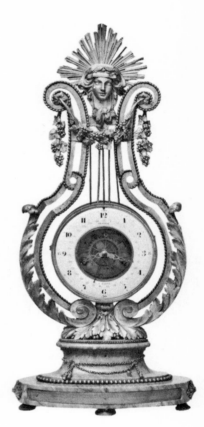

Fig. 206 Louis XV Clock with Case
of Bronze-Doré

Fig. 207 Lyre Form Clock.
Late 18th Century

Fig. 208 Louis XVI
Vase-shaped Clock

Fig. 209 Louis XVI Wall Clock with
Bronze-Doré Case

147

Nouveaux Liure de Boites de Pendulles de Coqs et Etuys de montres et autres necessaire au Orlogeurs.
Inventé par D. Marot Architecte avec Privilege.

Fig. 210 Design for a Clock by D. Marot

148

CHAPTER XVIII

Metalwares

HE metalwares of Old France experienced a precarious existence. Those of the base metals—iron, copper, brass, pewter, tin—were subjected to hard usage, and many succumbed. The precious metals—gold, silver-gilt and silver—were sent to the mints to be melted into coin to finance unsuccessful foreign wars during the reign of Louis XIV. The incendiary fires and destruction, which occurred during the French Revolution in the last years of the 18th Century, resulted in the loss of many masterpieces made by the goldsmiths during the prolific years of that century. Despite these hazards, enough survived to prove the right of the French metalist to take his place among the most gifted craftsmen of England, Germany, Italy and Flanders.

As in those countries, so it was in France, products made of metal performed two important services—utility and ornament, though these two functions frequently overlapped. Metalwares produced in the provinces may be grouped into five classifications: those used for cooking, heating, lighting, eating and decoration.

In the 17th Century when Henry IV originated the recipe for that delicious soup known as "Petite Marmite", cooking was done in the fireplace. But even after the introduction of the stove, the same stalwart iron pots and gleaming copper utensils continued to be popular, and remain so to this day. Great iron cauldrons which stood on three legs, or hung from iron cranes, were essential to every kitchen. In them simmered the delicious "pot-au-feu", characteristic dish of France, while from them in the southern provinces, the world-famous "Bouillabaisse" sent forth its enticing aroma. Trivets were also fashioned of iron and their lace-work was imaginative and beautiful. Copper was the favorite metal for a myriad of utensils—skillets, omelet-pans, stew-pans, milk-cans, water jugs and wall-fountains. Their forms are sturdy and forthright, their proportions delight the eye. The craftsmen decorated them with bands of brass with chasing and prickings, the designs being hearts, bouquets, leaves, and garlands.

Pewter was the preferred metal at table. Families of jugs for measuring were used when preparing food. For serving, plates, platters, porringers, pitchers, tureens, beakers and mugs, were used. Flatware was also made of pewter but far into the century spoons were the only eating tool, save for a man's own hunting knife, which served as his trusty companion which he used both as an aid to secure and to devour food. Pewter was the poor man's silver and in form and decoration it followed the patterns set by that precious metal. But it has a beauty of its own and deserves more than snobbish admiration.

Brass was also used at table but it was in articles for heating and lighting that the French developed this metal to a beauty never surpassed by the craftsmen of any other nation. Andirons, fenders, pokers, shovels, fire-screens and other tools for the hearth were made of brass. There were long-handled bed-warmers charmingly pierced and chased with hearts and flowers. To carry to church, and when coaching and sleighing, there were small square boxes which held live coals known as "muff-warmers".

When the fireplace progressed from the kitchen to the parlor and bedroom, its equipment was designed by the most accomplished artists and sculptors of the times. For one of the unique characteristics, and a basic reason for the advance of the decorative arts in France, was the fact that no artist, however great and famous, considered himself above the task of lending his genius to the creation of any decorative object, however trifling it might be. They set the pace and the provincial craftsmen did not loiter. Eagerly they took up the challenge and poured forth a host of beautiful wares that for centuries have commanded admiration.

Fireplace fittings adopted the style of their period. The massive lines of those made during the reign of Louis XIV were refined to greater elegance during the Régence which followed. Then they burst forth into the exuberance of the rococo.

Andirons were made of brass and of bronze in the form of swirls and scrolls. They were frequently surmounted with amours, or with a pair of figures such as a man and a woman in romantic pose dressed in the costume of the Louis XV period. The vogue for Chinoiserie was evidenced by Chinese figures among the scrolls. The Pompeian influence appeared in busts and arabesques. Throughout these times, fireplace equipment was remarkable for its fantasy, grace and for its charming beauty.

When décor passed on into the classic mood, fireplace fittings became architectural. The supports were like fluted columns topped with urns and similar classical motifs.

With the arrival of the Empire mode the trend was toward the massive. All the favored Napoleonic motifs were repeated—the caryatid, winged griffin, sphinx, while the embellishments showed laurel wreaths, husks, cornucopias.

Brass, bronze and bronze-doré entered the field of lighting fixtures to an important degree. Charming hand-lanterns were fashioned of pierced tin and were used by the peasants. The more fanciful of these were trimmed with bands of brass. Practically all the forms and motifs used during the 18th Century in silver were repeated in these baser metals. Candlesticks were made in a myriad of variations. There were candelabra, chandeliers, girandoles, wall-lights and handsome hanging lanterns.

Toward the middle of the 18th Century, a lighting fixture termed "Bouillotte" became popular. It consisted of two or three candleholders rising from one base, surmounted by a metal shade which was usually painted dark green. These were made with a rococo base, then with the fluted column and the delicate beading typical of the Louis XVI style and later were embellished with swans and other motifs of the Empire. About this time the use of oil for lighting became more general. Cisterns for holding the fluid were added to the forms originated for candles.

One of the most charming developments of the late 18th and early 19th Century was tole. Tole is painted tin. Black, green, red, mustard and a midnight-blue were the favorite ground-colors. They were embellished with over-paintings of flowers, Chinese scenes, and later were made in the forms and with the ornaments of the Empire. Candlesticks, lamps, lanterns, cache-pots, vases and boxes in many sizes, were fashioned of this ware. It was also used to encase clocks. Salvers, trays, coasters for carafes and many other forms of tableware were developed in tole. In fact one of the most characteristic developments in materials was this vogue for tole and for polished bronze.

There had been an increasing use of bronze for ornaments toward the end of the 18th Century. During the Empire, the fashion made a rapid stride forward. Polished to a brilliant sheen, bronze was used to fashion the entire case for clocks. Mantel garnitures were made of this metal and its use in lighting fixtures increased.

But it was in the realm of precious metals that the French best proved their genius. America is fortunate in having a collection of French silver of the 18th Century that is unsurpassed in the world, the gift of Catherine D. Wentworth of Santa Barbara, California to the Metropolitan Museum of Art, New York City. A study of this collection reveals the fertile invention, the delightful imagination, the brilliant execution, of the French goldsmith. Until recent times, the word "goldsmith" meant the worker in both gold and silver.

The guild of the goldsmiths was one of the first to be established and one of the longest to live of any of the guilds of France. It had its origin in the brotherhoods of craftsmen formed in the Middle Ages under the protection of Saint Éloi. Guilds were flourishing in many cities long before a decree was issued in 1543 which made the system compulsory. There were 178 such guilds functioning in 1785. Their members took a legally administered oath, and voted periodically in an election of a warden whose obligation it was to uphold and administer the statutes of the society.

The guilds operated an apprenticeship system. Eight years apprenticeship, and three years as a journeyman were requirements. Leniency in the required time of apprenticeship was extended to the sons of master-craftsmen. The candidate took frequent examinations, then was given a limited time to produce his "test-piece". In addition, he had to produce, in a few hours, an article of common usage, such as a cup or spoon. If he passed these tests successfully, he was given a final examination by the officials of the Mint. Then, as a master-craftsman, wearing his robes, he took an oath before these officials to carry on his craft with integrity and in accordance with the rules of the guild. He stamped three copper-plates with the personal mark he adopted and gave one to the Mint, one to the guild and kept one for his own record. It was the rule of both guild and Mint that every piece made by him or in his shop must carry this mark. Memberships in the goldsmiths guilds were limited and a candidate frequently had to wait even after successfully passing the tests, to be admitted as a master-craftsman.

The members of the Goldsmiths Guild were subject not only to the rules of their association, but also to the authority of officials appointed by the government to supervise the conduct of trade. Because goldsmiths worked in precious metals, they were under the jurisdiction of the officials of the Mints, which in the 18th Century were established in thirty-one cities in the provinces. Their headquarters was Paris. A system of marks was devised and rigorously policed. The collector will find an authoritative record of these marks in the book, *Guide to Old French Plate* by Louis Carré.

Silver is a versatile metal. It can appear sumptuous or simple. It is equally successful when its design depends upon linear proportions, when embellished with engraving, and when wrought in the three-dimensional style of the sculptor. It was in this later treatment that the French goldsmith evidenced his genius. He interpreted the ornate style of Louis XIV, the rococo style of Louis XV, the classic style of Louis XVI and the dramatic style of the Empire, with imagination and virility. Silver reached its most spirited and beautiful development under the direction of such men as Berain, Thomas Germain, Masson, Delaunay, Geraldon, Meissonnier, Forty, Auguste, Roettiers, Balzac and Salembier. The impetus given to the craft by these talented leaders, guided and inspired the provincial craftsmen to splendid achievement.

Candlesticks, candelabra, wall-lights, were made of silver and also a wide variety of tablewares. Flatware, platters, plates, pots and porringers; salvers, trays and cruet-stands; cups, beakers, bowls, ewers and basins, were designed throughout the 18th and early 19th Century in styles that followed those of architecture and decoration. The size and importance of the tureen invited the talent of the craftsmen to exercise the full flair of his talent and he was quick to seize the opportunity. Two forms, distinctly French, were developed—the wine-taster, which was a small bowl with one handle somewhat resembling a porringer in form and the "écuelle".

The *écuelle* was a low bowl with two handles and a cover. It stood on a saucer. The first editions of this piece show the cover as being flat, but it soon became repoussé and was topped with an ornamental finial. It occupies in French silversmithy the same position of importance as does the porringer in the American school and the teapot in the English fraternity.

The popularity of the table-top desk, whose form was originated by Boulle, invited the designing of ornamental writing equipment. The inkstand which included not only a well but a bell and a repository for quills, was made with its three parts united by a tray. Silver and silver-gilt were used for these, but bronze-doré or bronze combined with marble took precedence in the 19th Century.

The toilet table also created opportunity for the goldsmith. Beautiful boxes for powder and patches, vials for perfume, coffrets for jewels, mirrors, hair-dressing and manicure implements as well as tools for embroidery, were produced with amazing prodigality. Crystal, semi-precious stones, tortoise-shell and enamels were frequently combined with the metal in the production of these wares. A distinctive feature of these pieces during the days of Marie Antoinette was the combination of several shades of gold on one tiny patch-box or pomade jar.

There was still another field in which the French goldsmith scored a unique triumph. The beauty of Chinese porcelains was recognized throughout the nation as early as the 17th Century. This fashion was followed by a patriotic appreciation of the wares made in France at the factories of Sèvres, Chantilly, Saint-Cloud and Mennecy. The vases, bowls, candlesticks and statues which proceeded from the Orient and from the potteries of France were embellished with handsome mounts made of bronze and of gold and silver. The French craftsman exercised such exquisite taste, skill and imagination in his designs that this mating of ceramic and metal is a happy one.

Another phase of the metalist's talent is shown in the mounts made for furniture in brass, steel and bronze. In the palaces of the court, furniture mounts of bronze rose to an exquisiteness worthy of the jewelers' art. In the homes of the bourgeoisie and peasant, the fashion for emphasizing the importance of keys, keyholes, pulls and hinges, was continued but with characteristic simplification in design as well as in material. While the bronze mounts for palace furnishings were cast, then beautified and refined by hand-tooling, the mounts produced in the provinces were hand-wrought from sheets of metal. Of course, it was necessary to cast parts of the hinges and pulls, but they still retained their hand-wrought look. Toward the end of the 18th Century mounts declined in ornamental importance until the coming of the Empire style.

Fig. 211 Sketches for Silverware by Pierre Germain

Thetiere. 6.

Thetiere

Diverses Mosaiques à graver sur la Thetiere. 6.

Differents Ornements à graver sur les jattes.

Iatte profonde pour mettre vne Thetiere.

4.

A Paris chez I. Mariette rue St Iacques aux Colonnes d'Hercule.

Fig. 212 Sketches for Silverware by André Masson

Fig. 213 Silver Beaker with Cover.
18th Century

Fig. 215 Spoons. 18th Century

Fig. 214 Silver-gilt Écuelle by
Ludwig Imlen, Jr. Strasbourg,
Circa 1768

156

Fig. 216 Silver Coffee Pot, Decorated with Coffee Leaves, Berries and Spiral Fluting by Thomas Germain. Middle 18th Century

Fig. 217 Sugar Coaster by Nicholas Besnier. Circa 1728-1729

Fig. 218 Ewer, Silver on Brass. Early 18th Century. Silver Basin by B. Samson of Toulouse. Circa 1770

Fig. 219 Winetaster of Silver. Late 18th Century

Fig. 220 Silver Dish by B. Samson. Circa 1770

157

Fig. 221
Hot Water Urn of Silver-gilt and Gilt
Bronze. Made by Claude Odiot, 1798-1809

Figs. 222, 223
Coffee Pot and Tureen of Silver-gilt.
Made by Martin Guillaume Biennais,
1798-1809

Fig. 221

Fig. 222

Fig. 223

These pieces were probably given to his sister, Pauline, by Napoleon
upon the occasion of her marriage to the Prince de Borghese.

Fig. 224

Fig. 226

Figs. 224, 225, 226, 227
Vases of Porcelain and Semi-precious Stone
Mounted in Bronze-Doré in the Style of the
18th Century

Fig. 225

Fig. 227

159

Fig. 228 Tole. Early 19th Century

160

CHAPTER XIX

Lighting Fixtures

FROM the crude iron candlesticks and oil-lamps of the peasant, the French metalsmith developed a repertoire of lighting fixtures wrought in brass, bronze and silver which bespeaks the fertile imagination, amazing skill and the fine taste of Provincial craftsmen to an admirable degree. As in the case of furniture, the metalist of the provinces followed the styles established by the court, but intricate ornament gave place to a firm, vigorous line which emphasized without interruption the basic pattern.

During the period of Louis XIV the candlesticks and candelabra presented a vigorous scroll and massive baluster; this became more delicate and fanciful as the rococo style came into fashion and then was resolved into the simple, classic lines of the Louis XVI style. Then fluted balusters, neat beading, and taller, slimmer lines are characteristic of these fixtures. The Empire saw lighting fixtures of bronze, decorated with griffins, caryatids, swans, and stylized ornament. They often stood on claw feet.

A charming fashion in lighting fixtures was instituted during the Directoire and Empire; this was tole. The pieces followed the usual Empire forms and were made of tin or metal lacquered in green, royal-blue, red and mustard. They were ornamented with stencil-like paintings in gold, black or a contrasting color, the motifs being the favorite ones of the period.

161

Chandeliers and sconces during the 17th Century were made of brass and bronze with long, undulating arms occasionally interrupted by balls or knobs. To enhance the light given by the candles, lustres were used in more pretentious homes. During the time of Louis XIV, these lustres were large and flat with serrated edges. Later they became smaller in size and during the romantic era charming porcelain or faïence flowers were scattered among the metal branches.

The chandeliers of the Directoire and Empire periods show crisp, purposeful lines. The metal is drawn very thin and the surfaces are often chased. Chains and balls are used for ornament and also small lustres.

The use of oil was now more prevalent and lamps with an urn-shaped compartment for holding the fluid came into vogue. These lamps combined both metal and pottery and some of the most charming ones were made in tole.

Fig. 229
Louis XVI Wall Sconces

Fig. 230 Régence Wall Sconce

Fig. 231

Fig. 232

Fig. 233

Figs. 231, 232, 233
Candelabra. Middle and
Late 18th Century

Fig. 234
Candelabra of Bronze-Doré with
Porcelain Parrots and Flowers

Fig. 235
Lustre. Latter Half of the 18th Century

Fig. 236
Empire Candelabra of Silver-gilt

Fig. 237

Fig. 238

Figs. 237, 238, 239
Crystal Chandeliers. 18th and Early 19th Centuries

Fig. 239

Fig. 240 Hand-blocked Cotton Panel. Tree of Life Design. 1750-1800

CHAPTER XX

Textiles

THE four natural fibres of which cloth is made—wool, silk, linen and cotton—were developed in France to the zenith of their beauty.

When the Roman soldiers laid siege to the city in central France now known as Clermont-Ferrand, the women of the town mounted the walls and to appease the attackers flung down gold, silver, and lengths of "sayre". This cloth, woven of wool in a firm diagonal weave, rated equally with precious metals! Soon Caesar's conquering legions were clothed in this tribute cloth of Gaul—the *serge* that we wear now.

In the 17th Century Henry IV established the silk manufactory in Lyons, and there, during the reign of Louis XV, worked the greatest genius of all textile designers, Phillippe de la Salle. The glory of his designs has never been equalled.

Linen was developed not only by the loom but also by the skilled fingers of the lace-makers of Alençon, who created miracles of loveliness. Cotton, the last fibre to receive attention in France, has never been more charmingly presented than in the "toiles peintes" made during the last years of the 18th Century and the reign of Napoleon Bonaparte. The embroidery that the world knows, the Bayeux tapestry, was the work of Matilda and her ladies, while her husband, William the Conqueror, was away at war in England, so legend says. But of all the arts produced in France the greatest are those woven of wool—her glorious tapestries.

The romantic story of the textile trade is so much a part of France that it is retold in countless scenes throughout the land. The Great Clock of Rouen was given to the city by its prosperous Drapers Guild. It is large enough to span a street and the bombardments of two World Wars have not stopped it. In Orléans you may still walk along Great Scissors Street, Wool-Combers Street, and Street of the Hand That Spins. The magnificent stained glass windows of Amiens Cathedral were presented by the drapers and dyers who worked in that city around Thread Square. So important was the textile trade considered that scenes from the lives of its members were carved on the great Gothic Cathedrals. At Reims may be seen a sermon in stone. It is the story of the punishment of the dishonest draper who cut his cloth short.

When France began to weave is a mystery. The women were using a distaff and men had looms even when Julius Caesar arrived. The trade was considered so important that its members were enrolled into Guilds as early as the 13th Century. The rules were strict and rigidly enforced. The raw materials, the warp and woof, the finish, even the selvedge, were controlled by law. The hours of work, the number of looms, workers and apprentices a "Master" might have were all determined by the Guilds. When the watchman's horn blew, "sun-up" work was started and when the vesper-bell sounded, every loom instantly stopped or the Master went to jail. Inspectors appointed by the Guilds kept strict tab, and there was no recourse from their decisions and punishments. Despite the interference of kings and wars the Guilds controlled and policed the textile industry until the 19th Century when the innovation of the power-loom eventually developed the modern factory.

Though the historic records kept by the Guilds make interesting reading, those who love the texture, the color, the pattern, of textiles would much rather *see* what was produced during these centuries. One man kept this record. There are in Paris seven large volumes bound in green leather which bear the title *A Collection of Ribbons of 1632 To Be Used as a Sequel to the Book of Anecdotes of Our Time*. The collector? Cardinal Richelieu. This shrewd despot who, as Prime Minister, ruled France with an iron hand though sheathed in a silken glove, this astute diplomat who manipulated the destinies of all the nations of Europe, collected ribbons! Turn the pages of his seven books and the story of the looms of France is revealed by the bright samples more clearly than ever they could be told with words.

Cloth was scarce in France when home building started at the end of the destructive Religious Wars in the 17th Century. Henry IV, the new King, frankly said that he was the poorest dressed sovereign ever to be crowned and admitted that though he had twelve shirts, most of them were full of holes. When he announced that he had twelve handkerchiefs, his valet corrected him with a terse, "Only eight, Sire". One of the first projects Henry IV took upon himself after becoming King was the rehabilitation of the textile industry upon which so many people depended for a livelihood.

When the shuttles began to whirl they offered to the provincial home decorators—*serge, bourette, satinade* and *popeline.* These were all twill weaves made of wool or of wool or cotton combined with silk. There was also *basin,* a twilled cotton material with a narrow colored stripe.

Linen was woven in small geometric patterns of squares and diamonds and often had gay colored threads in the selvedge. Originally this was the trademark of the weaver, but it came to have a popular decorative value. In fact, the design of this narrow linen strip of cloth with bright colored selvedge persists in the dish-towels used to this day. In the early 18th Century linens appeared on the table, though sparsely. The King himself, Louis XV, had no table linen of his own—what he used, he rented!

Silks and velvets were used in the homes of the prosperous. The somber wool upholstery and draperies of the Louis XIII period gave place to damasks and brocatelle woven in large pomegranate, lace, leaf and vase patterns. The colors of the Louis XIV era were bright and rich, a glorious sun-yellow, ruby, a deep green. The Régence style introduced all-over patterns in a small scale, refined the large designs of the previous epoch and sponsored some of the most distinctive and beautiful patterns ever produced on French looms. Subtle colors such as slate-blue and plum were introduced. The threads used in these times were thick and gave the fabrics a rich texture.

Romance entered the loom with the Louis XV style. The patterns changed from stylized, dignified designs to realistic flowers of natural size. Colors were brilliant and threads were thinner.

The style Louis XVI emphasized thinner, lighter textiles. Small flower designs were placed between stripes and stripes themselves were popular. The colors were greyed. Thus fabrics followed the mood of classic restraint that dominated decorative art.

The Empire mode revolutionized both pattern and color. Brilliant monotone satins in emerald-green, sapphire-blue, citron-yellow became popular. Wide two-color stripes, reminiscent of Napoleon's martial days, were created. Designs in damasks were the bee, rosette, star, dot, urn, sometimes these were combined with stripes, and always they were formally and deliberately placed in the pattern.

During the 18th Century, the popularity of embroidery increased. Embroidery is a kind of textile which has its own special characteristics. It is usually accomplished by a thread carried by a needle over a finished foundation, but quilting, tucking, gathering and appliqué may also be considered as types of embroidery. It permits more originality of conception, more freedom of design, than weaving, knitting or printing, and notable is the fact that in practically every country in the world both men and women have expressed the ideology of their culture by means of embroidery. In the provinces of 18th Century France women advanced the art of embroidery to a high degree of originality, beauty and distinction. For the Frenchwoman had a rare gift for color and for design. She worked wonders with her pierced sliver of steel.

Just as the court set the fashions for furniture so it was with fabrics. Tapestries were the pride of the nobles, but their cost made them prohibitive to the middle-classes. The gifted French needlewoman was not to be outsmarted. She devised a method of re-producing the effect of tapestry with only coarse canvas, thread, needle, and work—endless work. In so doing, she, herself, created an art—petit point. Its beauty was lovely to see and it was amazingly durable. Not only cushions and chair coverings were created by this laborious stitchery but window valances, wall panels, entire bed-hangings and charming pictures.

Quilting was another form of needle-art applied to decorative fabrics. It beautified the surface and also served to combine two materials. This made for more durability in upholstery and for greater warmth in bed-coverings because layers of cotton or wool were often placed between the lengths of quilted cloth.

During the last half of the 18th Century printed cotton fabrics were increasingly used and revolutionized the decoration of the Provincial home. As before, this new fashion was started by the court but it swept through France with the speed of a forest fire. The fact that the manufacture and use of cotton was forbidden by law only seemed to increase the demand for it. Even the mistress of the King who made the prohibitive laws, bought them. Later, Josephine, wife of the Emperor Napoleon, adored them and she squandered more on clothes and decorations than Queen Marie Antoinette, denounced and beheaded for her extravagance, ever dreamt of spending. But perhaps the amazing popularity of the cotton prints was best explained by Rabelais when he commented, "How women love forbidden fruit!"

The name first given to these printed fabrics was "Indienne." For the source of their style was the Near East. In fact, names of Eastern origin continually punctuate the story of cotton textiles. The word itself "cotton" is derived from the Arabic name for the plant, "Kutn". The Persian city of Chiniz lent her name, only slightly changed by foreign pronunciation to "Chintz". Calico is an obvious adaptation of the Indian city, Calcutta. A book published in 1719 introduces this fabric as "A tawdry, pie-spotted, flabby low-priced thing called Calico, made by a parcel of heathens and pagans that worship the Devil and work for a half-penny a day." But what gay charm calico gives to a house!

Before *Indiennes* made their appearance in France, "crazy inventors" had been struggling to mechanize the making of cloth. Despite almost unsurmountable odds they achieved their purpose. It remained however for some clever person to devise a means of giving design and color to the drab, grey materials. It is said that a woman started it all with a letter. But we are getting ahead of our story.

In the time of Louis XIV the Dutch and Portuguese sailors and merchants had introduced the textiles of the Orient and of the Near East into France. Later, resentful of the high prices they charged for the precious wares, the King of France and his nobles resolved to form their own import company and the result was the organization of the Compagnie des Indies. One of the stockholders was the Marquise de Pompadour, infallible in her recognition of beauty and indefatigable in her acquirement of it. Among the many beautiful wares brought in were lengths of cotton of exquisite texture on which had been painted by hand, in varied and brilliant colors, the exotic fruits, flowers and birds of India. These painted cloth panels, ablaze with roses, peonies, carnations, chrysanthemums, anemones and pomegranates, created a sensation.

Down came the silks and velvets from windows and beds in the great chateaux; up to the store-room went the dull serge and heavy linens once prized in the cottages of the provinces. These new cottons were bright and gay. Every woman *must* have them. The weavers of wool and silk and velvet set up an awful howl. They put such pressure to bear on the King that he ordained that no cotton was to enter France, nor was cotton cloth to be woven on a French loom. No woman might wear this cursed cloth nor drape it in her home. But the next day his mistress appeared in a beautiful cotton dress! Backwards and forwards the pendulum swung for many years, then women and cotton won.

In 1757 a young German weaver newly arrived in France received a letter from a lady. It told him that a beautiful piece of *Indienne,* which she prized very dearly, had been ruined, could he duplicate it for her? This young man's name was Oberkampf, and he was clever and industrious. After endless night and day experiments with dyes and designs cut into wood-blocks, which he made in his little mill in the village of Jouy near Versailles, Oberkampf was at last successful. The ban on cotton had been lifted in 1759 so he presented to France and the world the cloth which became known as— "Toile de Jouy".

King Louis XVI and his Queen, Marie Antoinette, were frequent "Sunday drivers" and along with them went their children and aunts and cousins and the ladies and gentlemen of their court. One day they were amazed to see the fields near Versailles ablaze with color—it was as if a garden had bloomed overnight. Oberkampf was drying his *toiles de Jouy* in the sunshine. The Queen and her court went into ecstasies over the gay cloth, bought lavishly, and all France took up the vogue.

Naturally other manufacturers in other cities saw the profit possibilities of the new fashion and soon toiles were produced in many other cities in France. Gifted artists, such as Jean Baptiste Huet, were engaged to make designs for the new prints. A bloody revolution came, thousands were guillotined, but the fury passed and the printing of toiles continued, though now the designs incorporated the motifs of the new era. Then one day the Emperor, Napoleon, visited the little factory at Jouy, as had the King and Queen before him. When the Emperor saw the beauty of these textiles he took the jewelled star which decorated his own uniform and pinned it on the breast of Christophe-Phillipe Oberkampf.

Meanwhile the printing of cotton with wood-blocks having proven so successful the "crazy inventors" were again at work. They were in search of a way to produce printed cloth in greater quantity. They accomplished their purpose by engraving designs on large metal rollers and thereby hundreds of yards could be turned out in a single day. Every home throughout the provinces of France, like gardens after the passing of winter, burst into bloom.

The first designs to be printed on Oberkampf's toiles were small patterns. Then figures were interspersed with flowers and swags. The "Vintage", the "Four Seasons", "Balloon Ascension", "Famous Monuments", "Pleasures of Country Life", the "Five Continents", were the names of the designs which were applied in a single color—a rosy-red, blue, maroon, violet and occasionally a grey-black, and a mustard. As the interest in America took possession of France, Benjamin Franklin and Lafayette made their appearance on toiles. They were followed by William Penn and the American Indian, or rather what the French artist thought the American Indian looked like. These romantic designs were later discarded for classical and mythological scenes, and still later came the motifs favored during the Empire.

When polychrome (meaning many colors) printing was perfected and done on metal rollers, chintz came into its own. The old designs are, for the most part, flowers more or less realistically presented. At first these patterns were large in scale and clearly show the influence of India and Portugal. Later came Chinoiserie and still later came diminutive flowers in a vast variety of gay, quaint patterns. During the first years of the manufacture of printed fabrics, backgrounds for the designs were the natural color of the cloth itself. The flower prints brought with them the use of colored backgrounds, some of which were dark blue, red and even black.

The ingenuity of the French craftsmen, their taste and skill, is charmingly proven by the trimmings they created with threads. Fringes, tassels, gimps, and galloons evidence their fine color-sense and the fertility of their ideas.

There was a need to finish the ends of cloth so the weaver devised the idea of extending the warp threads beyond the edge of the length of cloth. These were bound and knotted together and formed a myriad of beautiful patterns. From this point it was but a step to create a separate fringe with a woven heading which was applied along the edge of the cloth.

A solidly woven band was called a "galloon"; a rounded band was known as a "cord"; a plaited or braided band which was sometimes ornamented with loops and tassels was given the name of "gimp". These trimmings had a functional purpose—to cover seams and joinings—but they also served to emphasize shape and line, and they added a decorative note to the object to which they were applied. Gimps, cords and galloons were used as a finish on draperies and to finish the upholstery on furniture where it met the wooden frame.

Another form of textile trimming employed by the French was the tassel. Its original purpose was probably to give weight to the cord from which it hung; they were also spaced on braids. Many of them are masterpieces of skill and intricate detail.

Lace is a descendant of embroidery. It developed from the application of fine stitches on linen but its existence cannot be traced before the 15th Century. It is said that Catherine de Medici and her daughter-in-law Mary Stuart, who was Queen of France and Scotland, introduced the use of cutwork and embroidered net to table linen and encouraged the use of lace edgings. At that time lace was imported from Italy and Flanders. When Henry IV wished to establish the making of lace in France his minister, Sully, told him, "What you need are iron and soldiers"—and so it was not until the end of the 17th Century that a lace-making industry was begun in France under Louis XIV and his minister Colbert.

Lace-makers were brought from Venice to teach the French and the first manufactory was established in Paris. The French lace-makers soon freed themselves of foreign tradition and developed a lace termed "Les Points de France" which came to excel the Italian laces in delicacy of workmanship and in fertility of design. However it was in the provinces—in the towns of Alençon and Argentan, and later in Valenciennes and Chantilly—where it really took root and flourished until the time of the Revolution in the closing years of the 18th Century.

It is fascinating to see how the minute threads followed the architectural styles of the decorative periods. The arabesques of Berain are duplicated. The design of the Sun

King, the sunburst, is seen among dolphins, martial trophies and mythological characters. Laces were made in designs obviously inspired by the beautiful marquetry of the cabinet-maker André Boulle.

When this symmetrical style was followed by the rococo we find the trend echoed in the laces. Flowers and birds appear and the popularity of Chinoiserie introduced figures, pagodas, peacocks, and miniature landscapes.

Marie Antoinette was a great devotee of lace. Her favorite flowers were the tulip, the carnation, but above all, the rose. They are seen entwined with ribbons and garlands, in the laces of her time.

Portraits painted during the 17th and 18th Centuries show a plentiful use of lace in costume. In the home it was used for bedspreads, bed-hangings, and draperies. But its most typical application in French décor was the embellishment of the dressing table with flounces of lace. A deep flounce extended from the top of the table to the floor. It was profusely gathered around three sides of the table. A second shorter flounce was placed over it. The top of the table was spread with lace. On it was grouped a standing mirror surrounded by pomade jars, perfume bottles and other accessories.

The majority of the fine ancient laces of France are in the hands of private collectors. There is a superb collection in the Metropolitan Museum of Art in New York City which is available for study.

Fig. 241 Ribbon of Satin Brocade. 18th Century

174

CHART OF PERIOD MATERIALS, COLORS AND MOTIFS

LOUIS XIV

Designs—Large stylized fruits and flowers—pomegranate, pineapple, sun-flower. Lace. Ferns.
Colors—Brilliant gold. Blue. Crimson. Plum.
Materials—Damask. Linen. Brocatelle. Needlework. Velvet. Wool.

LOUIS XV

Designs—Realistic flowers. Serpentine ribbons. Garlands. Plumes. Musical instruments.
Colors—Rich, mellow green. Blue. Yellow. Rose. Turquoise.
Materials—Brocade. Damask. Velvet. Texture weaves of silk, linen, cotton and wool.

LOUIS XVI

Designs—Small bouquets and flower-sprigs. Bowknot. Doves. Urns. Cupids. Pastoral scenes.
Garden implements. Stripes. Chinoiserie.
Colors—Lighter shades.
Materials—Taffeta. Brocades. Moiré. Printed cotton and linen.

EMPIRE

Designs—Swags, Bee, Rosette. Mythological figures. Bold stripes.
Colors—Emerald-green. Sapphire-blue. Citron-yellow. White.
Materials—Satin. Damask. Toiles. Chintz. Mull.

Fig. 242 Toile de Jouy. Linen, Red on White, Copper-plate Print,
Showing the Manufacture of These Fabrics. Circa 1783

Fig. 243 An Early Toile de Jouy, "Le Petit Buveau."
Linen, Wood Block Print, Red on White

Fig. 244 Pastoral Scene. Linen, Copper-plate Print,
Rose on White

Fig. 245 Printed Cotton with Classical Medallions. Designed by J. B. Huet. Circa 1805

Fig. 246 Floral and Chinoiserie Polychrome
Print on Linen. Circa 1780

Fig. 247 Floral Print; Red, White,
Black on Linen. Circa 1788

Fig. 248 Floral Print, Polychrome,
Linen. Circa 1785

Fig. 249 Polychrome Print on
Cotton. Circa 1790

Fig. 250 Velvet Brocade. 17th-18th Century

Fig. 251 Crimson Silk Damask. Early 18th Century

Fig. 252 Louis XV Silk Brocade

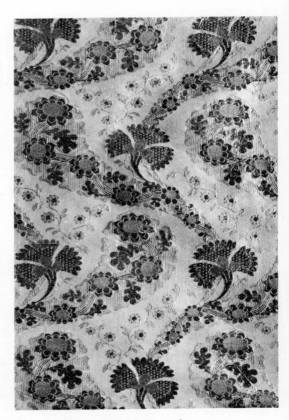

Fig. 253 Louis XV Silk Brocade

178

Fig. 254 Brocade. Middle 18th Century

Fig. 255 Silk. 3rd Quarter of the 18th Century

Fig. 256 Louis XVI Figured Silk

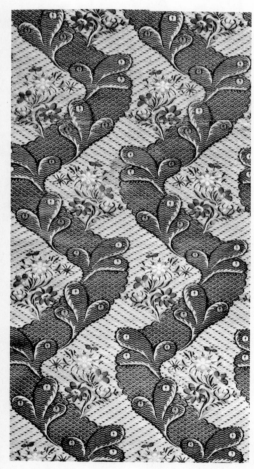

Fig. 257 Silk. 3rd Quarter of the 18th Century

Fig. 258 Satin Brocade Designed by Philippe de la Salle. Circa 1770

Fig. 259
Satin Brocade Coverlet Woven for Napoleon's Son. Circa 1811

Fig. 260
Satin Brocade Ordered by Napoleon
for the Palace of Fontainebleau

Fig. 261
Figured Silk with Design in Chenille.
18th Century

Fig. 262
Directoire Lampas

CHAPTER XXI

Ceramics

THE long reign of Louis XIV (1648-1723) began in depression, mounted to unprecedented glory, and ended in depression. Unsuccessful wars depleted the nation of money and men. Floods and famine impoverished the land. So desperate were the people that it is said children were eaten. In 1709 the treasury was exhausted. The King sent his gold table services to the Mint to be melted into coin. The nobles followed suit. But after this patriotic gesture they were faced with the practical problem of discovering a substitute.

The court turned to the crude crockery of the peasants. Within a few weeks' time the shops were denuded of their stock. The small potteries, which had, until now, pursued a precarious existence, were flooded with orders. A new fashion was born!

As early as the 15th Century, pottery had been made in France—mostly by adventurous Italians who learned the craft in their native land. A beautiful ware was produced in the time of Henry II (about 1525), which remains to this day one of the most noble of ceramic achievements. Today less than a hundred pieces of Henry II ware exist and even in its heyday not a great deal could have been made. A potter named Palissy (1510-1590) worked in the days of Catherine de' Medici, but though he valorously pursued his endeavor to master the craft, despite untold difficulty and extreme poverty, his experiments failed to establish a successful national industry.

The first pottery that continued to function in France for a considerable length of time was one which was founded about 1602 in Nevers as the hobby of an Italian nobleman who married a Frenchwoman. In the beginning, this pottery was directed by Italians but it eventually passed into the hands of local potters, and by hook or by crook, survived many lean years.

Toward the middle of the 17th Century (1643) the records show that a pottery was established in the north of France, in Rouen; another in Strasbourg. *Nevers— Rouen—Moustiers—Strasbourg—Marseilles*—these are names to remember. The wares which bear their name are among the most charming of ceramics.

When fashion created a demand for this ware, small potteries sprang up in villages throughout the land. Offshoots of Rouen were the potteries of Saint-Cloud, Sinceny, Quimper, Lille, who worked in the same decorative tradition. The success of Strasbourg resulted in new potteries in Lunéville, Bellevue, Longwy and Sceaux. These wares became known by the names of the cities in which they were founded, instead of by the names of their founders, as did the English wares, such as Spode, Wedgwood. Each pottery became celebrated for its special type of decoration, so that one can rightly designate the wares as the School of Rouen, the School of Moustiers, though it is hazardous to name the exact site of their manufacture. Their unique decorations were usually the origination of one man, one supreme artist who did, or did not, sign his pieces as his mood dictated.

In appearance and in substance French faïence is similar to that which Americans term "pottery". It was made of a red or yellow clay, coated with a thick, opaque, whitish stanniferous enamel. It was of a soft and porous texture and was not translucent. When it became lighter in weight and was improved with a lustrous lead glaze, its fine quality suggested that it was no longer adequate to call it by so crude a name as "pottery". A new name was coined—"faïence". Undoubtedly this name had its origin in a town in Italy long famous for its fine ceramics—Faenza. With a noble name, and with customers of taste and wealth, the faïence factories of France embarked upon a half-century (1700-1750) of glorious achievement, which they have never since equalled.

The ware of the first French faïence factory, Nevers, followed the Italian style of much over-painting and employed designs of biblical and mythological figures, then suddenly a charming origination was effected. This new type presented a cobalt blue body ornamented with flowers and birds sketched on splashily in white, or in white and yellow. These new designs were distinctly Persian in conception, though it is quite certain that the potters of Nevers never saw any Persian ceramics. However, as early as the 17th Century Chinese and Delft wares arrived in France, and they were the inspiration of a new phase in the history of the Nevers pottery. Nevers then produced a white ware decorated with Chinese adaptations rendered in a beautiful cobalt blue. But the quality of Nevers soon declined and during the 18th Century only coarse copies of other factories left this once distinguished pottery.

In Rouen the decorators sought inspiration from strange sources—bookbindings, lace, ironwork and embroideries. The borders on their wares are wrought in underglaze blue. The designs are arabesques and lambrequins of richness and distinction. As a "center" on these wares they would sometimes paint the armorial device of the family for whom it was made. Later they introduced Chinese scenes in the French taste.

New colors were added to the enameller's palette at Rouen. There was discovered a blazing, intense red, a brilliant green, and a rich ochre yellow. These were combined with the original royal-blue color. The embroidery-like designs were filled in with these polychrome colors and the result was a jewelled mosaic-brilliance. It is delightful to imagine a table set with plates, platters, pitchers, vases, candlesticks, tureens, of such handsome ware. Madame de Sévigne, author of the letters that so delightfully chronicle these times, wrote to her daughter, after a visit to Provence, complimenting the beauty of a table set with faïence, though she was accustomed to the sumptuous silver and gold tableware used at the court of Louis XIV.

While the wares of Rouen were rich, formal, colorful, a new type of decoration, equally beautiful and of greater delicacy and elegance, was originated in Moustiers. Here again the color was blue, but it was a lighter, a sapphire, almost an azure, blue. Delicate traceries of this charming color presented garlands and scrolls, hanging canopies, decorative pedestals, among which were cupids and satyrs. At Moustiers, wares decorated in a mustard color and in a reseda green were also produced. The fine quality of Moustiers continued far into the next reign when, records show, a complete service was made for that woman of exquisite taste, the Marquise de Pompadour.

Ceramics had been made around Strasbourg since the days of the Romans but in 1709 the pottery came under the direction of Paul Hannong who devised an entirely new method of decoration which was destined to influence all of the faïence of France. Hannong, who was to be recognized as one of the greatest ceramic painters of all time, fired his ware in the usual way, but he placed it a *second* time in the kiln. This second firing was a light firing—the temperature never mounting to the intense heat of that required to fuse the substances of the faïence. It only served to melt into the ware the transparent enamels with which he painted his decorations. Consequently, a wonderful new palette was made available to the ceramic painter. His brush was dipped into a rainbow of colors.

The Strasbourg ware was remarkable for its lightness, the glaze was smooth, lustrous and milk-white; the shapes were fanciful and vigorous; the effect was one of charm and originality. To blue, red and green, Hannong added a rich magenta, a delicate mauve, a brilliant emerald-green, a charming range of pinks. After the first firing the design was sketched on with black, but these lines no longer became fuzzy and grey from intense heat, they remained crisp and clear. Hannong was the first to gild faïence and this development so delighted Louis XV that he ordered an entire service.

Meanwhile the potteries in Saxony, established for the making of porcelain, or china, as Americans call the ware, had developed an accomplished school of flower-painters. Inspired by their work, Hannong proceeded to decorate faïence with a porcelain-type of technique. Under his genius it was more than mere copying; while he accepted the idea of the flower decoration, he interpreted it with the casual grace, with a freedom and vigor, that was harmonious with faïence.

This Strasbourg ware was an instantaneous success. It gave new life to the industry. Not only table and small decorative wares were made, but great vases, clock-cases, pedestals, even stoves were produced. Of rococo design, embellished with colorful bouquets, the forms have a glorious feeling for the inherent plasticity of clay. While the brilliant colors of their embellishments and vigorous borders fairly sing.

Other potteries followed Hannong's lead. At Sceaux and at Marseilles, the porcelain-technique of decoration was pursued even further. Delicate scenes of gardens and landscapes were combined with flowers and foliage. All characterized by a charming delicacy. During the brief span of fifty years French faïence reached its zenith.

The makers of porcelain became alarmed by the popularity of faïence. They began to invoke the law to prevent its production. England had become aware of the demand for faïence and was beginning to export the cheap ware in quantity into France as early as 1735. Soon beautiful French faïence ware was to descend to the level of mere novelties for the souvenir hunters. Political emblems and scenes were crudely painted on it. The ware itself became coarse. It had a brief resurgence during the early 19th Century when a plain colored cream ware decorative in shape and light in weight, was produced. Occasionally the body color of this ware was a strong canary yellow or a rich sepia. The decoration was chiefly single color flowers, scenes of Paris and mythological subjects. It was charming but lacked the distinction of the queenly wares of Rouen, the elegance of Moustiers and the fresh vitality of Hannong's Strasbourg. During its brief heyday French faïence achieved beauty that was rare. It remains a lost art, still unappreciated, despite the increasing number of ceramic collectors in America.

It was Madame Pompadour who became enamoured of the beautiful porcelain produced in Saxony, and who insisted that a factory for its manufacture be established

184

in France. The result was the founding of the Royal Manufactory of Sèvres and of Vincennes. These were later followed by the establishment of porcelain potteries at Saint-Cloud, Mennecy and Chantilly. Workmen, who professed to know how china was made, were imported, but for a long time their efforts were unsuccessful and the secret remained in Saxony, where it had been discovered in 1709 by a chemist named Boettger.

Though unable to reproduce Boettger's "true china", the French potteries created a ware known as "soft-paste" which is exquisitely beautiful. The texture of this soft porcelain is so fine and close as to appear velvety. The enamel of the decorations, which were applied with exquisite restraint, became so completely fused with the body of the ware, that no visible difference can be seen between the virgin and the painted surface. This is never true of hard porcelain, whose decorations seem to rest on the surface, and to have a different texture which conflicts with its lustre.

Magnificent colors were produced at Sèvres, whose names must be a part of the vocabulary of every one interested in the decorative arts. There was a cobalt blue called "bleu-de-roi"; a beautiful pansy color called "violet pensée"; a pale jonquil yellow and apple green, and a vibrant grass-green called "vertpré"; a sky-blue called turquoise; a rose Pompadour, so named in honor of the founder; a lighter shade called rose Du Barry, for the mistress who succeeded the Marquise du Pompadour in the affections of the King, Louis XV.

The mark of Sèvres is two Ls intertwined, under this is placed a letter A denoting the year 1753. The letters of the alphabet proceed chronologically up to 1777, when they become AA in 1778, but they end with OO which denotes the year 1792. Then production was ended by the Revolution until the factory was reopened by Napoleon.

Fig. 263 Bisque Ornaments. 18th Century

Fig. 264

Figs. 264, 265, 266
Faïence of Rouen. 18th Century

Fig. 265

Fig. 266

Fig. 267

Fig. 268

Figs. 267, 268
Faïence of Moustiers. Early 18th Century

Fig. 269 Nevers Vases

Fig. 270

Figs. 270, 271, 272, 273
Faïence of Strasbourg. 18th Century

Fig. 271

Fig. 272

Fig. 273

188

Fig. 275

Figs. 275, 276
Porcelain of Chantilly and Mennecy

Fig. 274 Marseilles Vase

Fig. 276

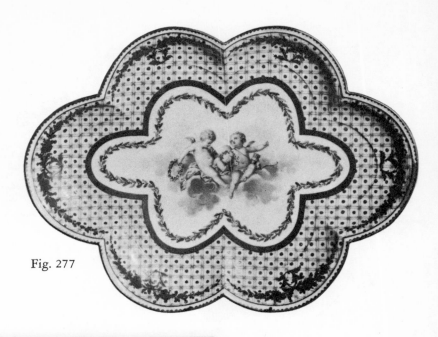

Fig. 277

Fig. 278

Figs. 277, 278, 279
Sèvres Porcelain

Fig. 279

Fig. 280

Fig. 281

Fig. 280 Cache-pot. 18th Century

Fig. 281 Vases. 18th Century

Fig. 282 Empire Coffee Service

Fig. 282

191

Fig. 283 Designs for Cups by Fay. Late 18th Century

CHAPTER XXII

Wall Coverings

HE walls of the homes of France were first covered with whitewash, which was later replaced by paint. The walls of the palaces were first hung with tapestries in which the looms of the Gobelins, Aubusson and Beauvais achieved unequalled beauty. Tapestries gave place to wood and wood to fabric and then came wallpaper whose comparatively modest price made it available to many.

One of the most notable achievements of the French craftsmen was wood-panelling which was termed "boiseries". From floor to ceiling, the walls were covered by a succession of panels. Doors, mantels and windows continued their design and thus a harmonious effect was achieved. These wooden-panels were sometimes set with mirrors, with fabric and canvas panels painted in oil.

The *boiseries* of the Régence are remarkable for their refined elegance. The favored woods were oak and walnut. Panels of beautiful proportion were ornamented, top and bottom, with light carvings of shell and foliage motifs. A firm crisp, serpentine line distinguishes the panels of the Louis XV period while those of the Louis XVI era show fine moldings and carvings of the popular motifs of musical instruments and arabesques. During the later 18th Century the wood was frequently lacquered in light tones of grey and green, occasionally parts of it were marbled. During the Empire the walls were plastered and painted and in the more luxurious homes the ceilings were richly decorated with colorful murals.

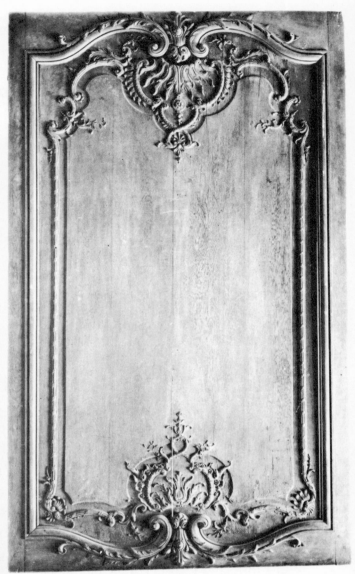

Fig. 285 Panel. Late 17th or Early 18th Century

Fig. 284 Carved Oak Door. 17th or
Beginning of the 18th Century

194

Fig. 286 Louis XV Door Panel

Fig. 287 Louis XVI Carved Wood Panel

But wood and fabric were beyond the budgets of any save the wealthy and in the early years of the 18th Century a vogue developed for Domino papers. These were small paper panels printed by the wood-block process by a group of men called "Dominotiers", their name being derived from the French word "domino" which means "images". They originated the idea of decorated paper applied to walls and worked from 1550-1600, but their names are not known. The crude panels that they made were decorated with squares and checks amongst which figures—frequently equestrienne—appeared in medallions. The peasants and bourgeoisie seized upon them eagerly and used them as a decoration over mantels.

The Dominotiers had a difficult time for the printers and booksellers became jealous of their success and had rigorous laws passed which confined their productions to small sized panels. These laws retarded the development of wallpaper, but not for long. Though wallpaper was a bastard industry—being merely an imitation of tapestries and of fabric—and imitations usually remain spurious—the French craftsmen by reason of their inventiveness, skill and taste raised it from lowly beginnings to a state of honor. Wallpaper came to be recognized as one of the most charming products of their genius.

The most accomplished artists of their times enlisted themselves in the development of wallpaper. When touched by the genius of Boucher, Huet, Fragonard, Lafitte, Robert, it is not surprising that the industry took wings. The creative ability of the artist was matched by the courage and invention of men such as Papillon, Chauvau, Reveillon, Jacquemart and Benard, who established shops and factories dedicated to this offshoot of the respected textile trade.

In the beginning, the industry flourished chiefly in Normandy which was the home of large paper mills, but it soon spread to Paris, Lyons, Orléans, Macon and other important centers. The simultaneous development of the printing process gave impetus to the production of wallpaper. At first it was laboriously printed with wooden-blocks, then colored by hand. Gradually the use of the roller and of printing in successive colors was introduced and finally Nicholas Louis Robert of Essones invented a means of printing paper in long stripes which could be joined almost invisibly. As men learned to build and to manage bigger printing presses, large panels measuring as much as ten feet tall and several yards long were produced.

About 1727 domino papers began to have a hardy rival in the marbelized papers whose intricate making called for the skillful use of great feathers. These were followed by "flock" papers. The designs of these papers were large and stemmed from damasks. Over their surface (to which glue had been applied) bits of wool were blown. It adhered to the paper and the result was an interesting texture effect. About 1750 the use of bits of wool was superseded by silk and still later by brilliant grains of gold and silver.

The ships that came from the Orient brought fabric panels from India which were hand-painted with designs of birds and flowers. Among the sea chests these vessels brought from China lengths of hand-painted papers which showed flowers and land-scapes. The popularity of these importations suggested new designs to the wallpaper manufacturers of France. They quickly reproduced them on their wares and when the Marquise de Pompadour bought these papers to decorate her rooms at Versailles, the new fashion was launched.

The stylized designs suggested by Oriental imports gave place, about 1780, to typical Louis XV patterns. Realistic flowers, swags and garlands became the vogue. Decorative birds such as pheasants appeared among the flowers. Many landscape scenes where romantic figures disported themselves among the blossoms were produced. These patterns flowed over the surface of the paper with buoyancy and grace. Toward the end of the century wallpaper patterns followed the trend of all furniture and ornament and adapted the classic restraint characteristic of the Louis XVI style. The flowers no longer bloomed in careless profusion but were contained in baskets and vases, which were neatly confined by stripes and swags. The fanciful artist Pillement scored a popular success with his Chinoiserie designs just as the mode for the Pompeian medallion and arabesque was later greeted with enthusiasm.

The Revolution, a Dark Age for so many of the crafts of France, did not retard the output of wallpaper. It was not considered a luxury industry but a democratic one, and so it was permitted to flourish without restraint while the production of fine fabrics, china, silver and other decorative arts was at a standstill. Then wallpapers presented the triumph of Liberty among medallions of revolutionary trophies and this was followed by designs showing classical figures, urns and arabesques.

The colors employed in the wallpapers of the Louis XV and Louis XVI periods were pastels in bright but gentle hues. They echo the tones of the fabrics of these periods. But when the Empire period came in, the colors became bold and bright, just as did the textiles of this epoch. Chalk-white was combined with emerald-green, citron-yellow and red with dramatic effect. A typical design of the Empire era was drapery patterns. These show folds of material gathered in panels and swags and held by rosettes. Borders of stylized designs were applied on the walls either as extra strips or were a part of the paper itself.

The highest technical achievement in the wallpapers of the early 19th Century were the large panels showing landscape scenes in which appear figures in modish costumes, brilliantly colored marine papers and grisaille panels presenting mythological subjects. Toiles and many other types of fabrics were reproduced on wallpaper which continued to be influenced by textile fashions. The industry reached its peak in the production of series of panels such as "The Five Senses", "Paul and Virginia", "The Incas" and "Telemachus".

Wallpaper was used in a number of ways other than that of being applied to walls. It was used on fireboards and appeared in over-door panels. It was inserted in frames and placed over mantels, along beds, around mirrors. Screens were fashioned of it. The Chinoiserie designs and scenic patterns were favored for this purpose. And it is interesting to note that the first person to record the history of this delightful phase of the decorative arts of Old France was an American—Nancy McClelland.

Fig. 288 Chinoiserie Wall Panel of Painted Silk

Fig. 289
A fragment of "The Five Senses" issued by Revillon during the latter part of the 18th Century. It is beautifully drawn and possesses delightful charm and superb decorative feeling. The background is muted green-blue, the figures are grisaille.

Fig. 290 Polychrome Wallpaper in the Style of Pillement

Fig. 291 Wallpaper. Late 18th Century

Fig. 292 Overdoor Panel of Wallpaper

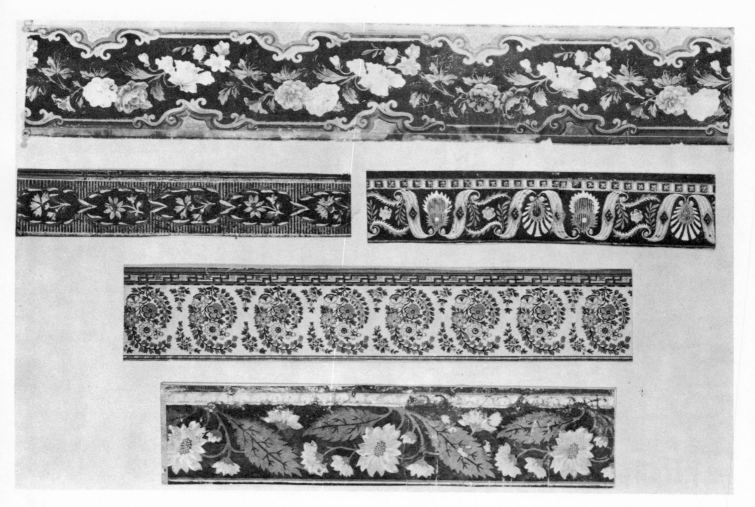

Fig. 293 Borders of the Early 19th Century

Fig. 294 Wallpaper Showing Pastoral Scene
in the Manner of Toile

201

Fig. 295 Paper Panel for a Fireboard.
19th Century

Fig. 297 Wall-paper. 19th Century

Fig. 296 Wallpaper Showing a
Gardener. Circa 1795-1800

202

CHAPTER XXIII

Floor Coverings

WEET scented herbs were strewn among the straw and rushes, or flung over the sand that covered the floors in the first-built homes of Old France. For the floors, being made of stone or tile, were hard and cold. Later this custom was discontinued in favor of small mats woven of rushes. These little mats were placed beside the bed to protect the feet from the cold floors when rising and were called "descentes de lit". Their crude comfort proved so welcome that small mats—oval, square or round—were also placed before chairs. When one moved his chair about, the mat was moved too.

As the desire for comfort increased, rushes were woven into mats large enough to cover the entire room, and later a flat straw matting was devised and laid in strips upon the floor. It was woven in simple, geometric designs in one or two colors. The skins of animals were also used and after textiles became more readily available, woolen scraps were carefully hoarded and sewn into patchwork mats. This was about all the underfoot luxury known in homes until far into the 18th Century. Rugs were possessed only by Kings. An old print shows that even Louis XIV had no carpet in his bridal chamber.

With the coming of the 18th Century a fashion for hardwood floors arrived. But hardwood was rare and precious. Only the prosperous could afford it. Its high cost caused it to be selected with care and it was handled with the skill and invention

203

usually accorded costly material. The prized bits of wood were sawed, matched, harmonized, smoothly sanded and fitted into intricate patterns. The owner was too proud of possessing a wooden floor to cover it with carpet. Yet rugs had been woven in France before the time of Charlemagne.

In 732 A.D. the Saracens invaded France and were defeated by Charles Martel, father of Charlemagne, in a battle near Aubusson, a little town on the river Creuse about two hundred miles south of Paris. Many of these soldiers settled there and began to weave rugs, a craft learned from their Oriental ancestors. They said that the waters of the little river, which flows through the center of the village, was peculiarly effective in "fixing" dyes. From this meager beginning the craft spread to the towns of Felletin and Bellegarde. When Henry IV was fighting his way to the throne (1689) these two cities were among the first to recognize him as their sovereign. In appreciation of their loyalty he took the weavers of the Aubusson group under his protection. Laws were passed forbidding the importation of rugs and tapestries, and they prospered. The industry passed under royal direction with Louis XIV on the throne and Colbert, Finance Minister to the King, sent experienced dyers, and great artists, to improve their weavings. Soon the name "Aubusson" won recognition and fame throughout the world, a supremacy it continues to enjoy.

The rugs of Aubusson have several unique characteristics. Though the manufactory enjoyed royal direction and patronage, the output was not confined to the King and his court. It was available to the middle-classes. Though of Oriental origin, their weavers quickly broke with tradition and created a design, color, and technique that was distinctly French. The designs echoed the styles of the national decorative periods—the elaborate style of Louis XIV; the fanciful rococo of Louis XV; the classic restraint of Louis XVI and the formal, dramatic spirit of the Empire. In weave they followed the technique of the great tapestries produced in France and which are her greatest glory.

Aubusson rugs are not woven from top to bottom, as are oriental rugs. They are woven sideways. Both a high and a low warp loom are used. Both sides are alike, though usually the reverse side reveals more threads. The warp threads are of cotton; the weft threads are of wool or of polished worsted. They have no fringe. The selvedge is turned under and the rug is lined. They have a distinctive texture which is firm and flat and they are quite thin. Therefore these weavings were used not only as floor coverings but also for upholstery. Rugs and upholstery of this type were woven in other cities than that of their origin but they are always called "Aubusson", just as the rugs of thick pile are termed "Savonnerie".

The Savonnerie, named because it was made in an old soap factory in Chaillot, is the royal rug of France. Its manufacture was begun by John Fortier in 1601, but in 1604 Pierre Dupont claimed to have invented the process and presented a report to Henry IV which so impressed the King that he brought Dupont to the Louvre to make rugs for the court. Dupont soon found that he needed help and took as his partner Simon Lourdet. When larger quarters were needed, Dupont continued to work in the Louvre, and Lourdet set up a branch in an old soap factory, a part of which also served as a home for children. It was a shrewd arrangement because it assured both space and cheap labor.

The children were apprenticed for twelve years. The Home received a small fee for each child's work during the last eight years of apprenticeship, and at the end of the term every child was trained to a highly skilled trade and received a small amount of money.

The business prospered through the years and eventually both Dupont and Lourdet were succeeded by their sons. The crowded quarters at the Louvre were abandoned for a large factory in Chaillot—once a suburb of Paris but now an aristocratic section of the beautiful metropolis. Le Brun and many of the great artists of France were commissioned to design the rugs. The entire output was reserved for the King and fabulous prices were paid for them.

Savonneries are characterized by a deep, rich pile. The warp threads are usually linen and the weft threads are wool. The pile is formed by tying separate knots across the warp over a sharp-edged iron rod which extends across the width of the weaving. When a row is ended, this sharp tool is removed and as it is drawn out, the wool is cut. The tufts are evened by a second cutting. Then the surface is smoothed down around the design and thus a carved or embossed effect is achieved.

The early Savonneries show a remarkably fine weave and close pile. The oldest one to be preserved was woven for Cardinal Richelieu and may be seen in Paris today. The design is elaborate, the coloring is dark, and is remarkable for the predominance of black. Another old Savonnerie which has been preserved was made for Ann of Austria, mother of Louis XIV, and has a rusty-black background.

The designs of the Louis XIV period were wrought in rich, brilliant color. The patterns are architectural in plan and show elaborate scrolls, acanthus foliage, martial trophies, the characteristic sunburst motif and royal insignia.

Pastel colors, designs of realistic flowers and musical emblems were introduced during the time of Louis XV. These were superseded during the Louis XVI era by designs which combined garlands, ribbons, bouquets and trophies with classic borders.

Though the manufacture of Savonneries was discontinued during the Revolution, the craft was revived by Napoleon. Cornucopias, martial trophies, the bee and the imperial initial "N" appear in them. The colors are brown, with turquoise and red; green with gold and with red.

A third type of carpet was produced in France during the late 18th Century and used in the homes of the middle-class. It was called "moquette". These rugs were small and intended to be placed by the bed or scattered about the room. In weave the *moquette* resembled the machine-made axminster. Small rugs were also made of petit point and gros point and were placed in luxurious bedrooms and boudoirs.

In almost every country but France simple rugs and carpets were woven by the peasants and used by the middle-classes in their homes. In old France, carpets and rugs were strongly allied to the great art of tapestry and remained an exclusive and precious possession of King and court. The genius of the creative artist was generously expended on their design, their weaving was ever the province of highly skilled craftsmen, and no expense was spared in their production. When the King wished to make an important present to a foreign ruler, his choice was invariably an Aubusson or Savonnerie carpet. Occasionally the factories were permitted to accept commissions from other courts which paid fabulous prices for these rare and unique possessions. Thus the industry, though constricted, progressed under circumstances that maintained a high measure of quality in design and execution and which caused the rugs of Old France to be one of the most beautiful expressions of the weavers' craft.

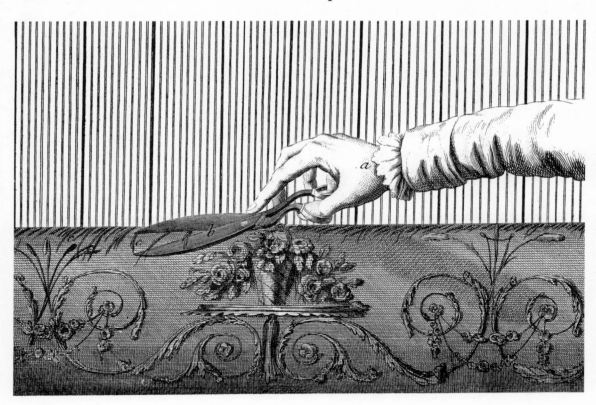

Fig. 298 Savonnerie Rug. Early 18th Century

Fig. 299 Aubusson Rug. Middle 18th Century

Fig. 300 Aubusson Rug Woven for the Country Home of the Marquis de Marigny, Brother of Madame du Pompadour

Fig. 301 Aubusson Rug. Late 18th or Early 19th Century

Acknowledgments

Americans have evinced such a keen appreciation of French Provincial Decorative Arts that many important documents and products of this school have been brought to this country and are housed here in museums and private collections. Therefore, I have deliberately chosen the illustrations of this book from American sources. Of course, no complete study can be made without spending much time in the country of their origin, but this opportunity is possible only to a fortunate few. The prodigal productivity of France and the taste and persistence of American dealers and collectors have created a rich fund for research which may be enjoyed without overseas travel.

I wish to acknowledge, with appreciation, permission to reproduce the illustrations shown here to the following:

BOSTON MUSEUM OF FINE ARTS, BOSTON, MASS.
FIGURES: 48; 50; 52; 58; 72; 90; 174; 176; 235; 254; 264; 269; 274; 280; 281.

THE ART INSTITUTE OF CHICAGO, CHICAGO, ILL.
FIGURES: 4-9; 55; 266; 267; 268; 270-273.

THE DETROIT INSTITUTE OF ARTS, DETROIT, MICH.
FIGURES: 21; 36; 82; 96; 132; 137; 142; 147; 148; 150; 151; 158; 160; 163.

THE MONTREAL MUSEUM OF FINE ARTS, MONTREAL, CANADA
FIGURES: 133; 135; 139; 143-145.

COOPER UNION MUSEUM OF DECORATIVE ART, NEW YORK, N. Y.
FIGURES: 169; 288; 290; 291; 293-297.

FRENCH & COMPANY, NEW YORK, N. Y.
FIGURES: 15; 17; 28; 85; 112.

JOSEPHINE HOWELL, NEW YORK, N. Y.
FIGURES: 164; 165; 166.

EDWIN JACKSON, NEW YORK, N. Y
FIGURES: 170-173.

ELINOR MERRELL, NEW YORK, N. Y
FIGURES: 167; 202; 228.

THE METROPOLITAN MUSEUM OF ART, NEW YORK, N. Y.
FIGURES: 1; 16; 18; 26; 27; 38; 42-47; 49; 51; 53; 56; 59; 68; 69; 94; 109; 114; 117; 122-124; 130; 183-185; 187-190; 192-194; 196-201; 213-223; 236; 240-253; 255-262; 265; 284-287.

Bibliography

GENERAL

French Interiors, Furniture, Decoration
  by T. A. Strange; Charles Scribner's Sons, N. Y.

History of France
  by François Pierre Guillaume Guizot; Estes & Lauriat, Boston.

French Furniture and Decoration in the 18th Century
French Painters of the 18th Century
French Architects & Sculptors of the 18th Century
French Engravers & Draughtsmen of the 18th Century
  by Lady Dilke; George Bell & Sons, London.

Seventeenth Century, Letters, Sciences and Arts
Eighteenth Century, Letters, Sciences and Arts
  by Paul Lacroix; Firmin Didot, Paris.

Pompeiana
  by Sir William Gell and John P. Gandy; Chatto & Windus, London.

La Vie Populaire a Paris au XVIII Siècle
  by Marguerite Pitsch; A. et J. Picard et Cie, Paris.

Modes and Manners
  by Max von Boehn; J. B. Lippincott Company, Philadelphia.

Dictionaire des Sciences et les Arts Liberaux
  by Diderot et L'Alembert; Paris 1777.

ARCHITECTURE

Small French Buildings
  by Lewis A. Coffin, Jr., Henry M. Polhemus, Addison F. Worthington; Charles Scribner's Sons, New York.

French Provincial Architecture
  by Phillip Lippincott Goodwin; Henry Oothovt Milliken; published in New York.

Twenty-five Great Houses of France
  by Sir Theodore Andrea Cook; Country Life, London, England.

FRENCH PROVINCIAL DECORATIVE ART

CERAMICS

La Porcelaine de Sèvres
by Édouard Garnier; Maison Quantin, Paris.

Recueil de Faïence Français dite de Henri 11 et Diane de Poitiers
by Henri et Carle Delange; Paris.

French Pottery and Porcelain
by Henri Frantz; Charles Scribner's Sons, New York.

Repertoire de la Faïence Française
Editors: Mm. le Docteur Chompret, Jean Bloch, Jacques Guerin, Paul Alfassa; Serge Lapina; Paris 1933.

French Faïence
by M. L. Solon; Cassell and Company, London.

Marks and Monograms on European and Oriental Pottery
by William Chaffers; Borden Publishing Co., Los Angeles, Calif.

FLOOR COVERINGS

European and American Carpets & Rugs
by Cornelia Bateman Farady; Dean-Hicks Co., Grand Rapids, Mich.

FURNITURE

Les Ébénistes du XVIII Siècle
by Comte François de Salverte; G. Van Oest et Cie, Paris and Bruxelles.

Le Meuble Français d'Après les Ornamanistes de 1660 á 1789
by Comte François de Salverte; G. Van Oest, Paris.

French Provincial Furniture
by Henri Longnon and Frances Wilson Huard; J. B. Lippincott Company of Philadelphia.

Le Siège en France du Moyen Age a Nos Jours
by Paul Hartmann, Paris.

Le Meuble—Ameublement Provençal et Comtaden
by L'Abbé G. Arnaud D'Agnel; Lucien Laveur, Paris.

Le Mobilier Louis XV au Musée des Arts Décoratif de Paris
by Egon Hessling; Libraire D'Architecture et Des Arts Décoratifs, Leipzig.

Louis XIV and Régence
by Seymour de Ricci; William Helburn, Inc., New York.

Le Style Louis XVI
by Seymour de Ricci; Hachette et Cie, Paris.

Collection de L'Art Régional en France
L'Habitation Basque by Louis Colas
Le Mobilier Basque by Louis Colas
Le Mobilier Alsacien by Paul Gélis
Le Mobilier Vendéen by J. Gauthier
Le Mobilier Provençal by Henri Algoud
Le Mobilier Bressan by Alphonse Germain
Le Mobilier Breton by Paul Banéat
Le Mobilier Flamand by Victor Champier
Le Mobilier Bourguinon by G. Jeanton
Le Mobilier Lorrain by Ch. Sadoul
Le Mobilier Normandy by Léon Le Clerc
Le Mobilier Auvergnant by J. Gauthier

INTERIORS

Intérieurs Rustiques
Edited by Charles Moreau, Paris.

FRENCH PROVINCIAL DECORATIVE ART

Les Boiseries du Musée Carnavalet
by François Boucher; Charles Mareau, Paris.

SILVER

A Guide to Old French Plate
by Louis Carré; Chapman and Hall, London.

TEXTILES

Painted and Printed Fabrics
by Henri Clouzot; Yale University Press, New York.

Philippe de la Salle
by Belle M. Borland; University of Chicago Press, Chicago, Illinois.

The Bayeux Tapestry
by André Lejard; Artra, Brugière, Fournier, Lang & Blanchong, Paris.

The Romance of French Weaving
by Paul Rodier; Frederick A. Stokes Company, New York.

La Toile Imprimée
by Henri-René D'Allemagne; Librairie Gründ, Paris.

WALL COVERINGS

Histoire du Papier Peint en France
by H. Clouzot et Ch. Fallot; Charles Mareau, Paris.

Historic Wallpapers
by Nancy McClelland; J. B. Lippincott Company, Philadelphia.